# The Twitter Presidency

CH01507743

*The Twitter Presidency* explores the rhetorical style of President Donald J. Trump, attending to both his general manner of speaking as well as to his preferred modality. Trump's manner, the authors argue, reflects an aesthetics of white rage, and it is rooted in authoritarianism, narcissism, and demagoguery. His preferred modality of speaking, namely through Twitter, effectively channels and transmits the affective dimensions of white rage by taking advantage of the platform's defining characteristics, which include simplicity, impulsivity, and incivility. There is, then, a structural homology between Trump's general communication practices and the specific platform (Twitter) he uses to communicate with his base. This commonality between communication practices and communication platform (manner and modality) strikes a powerful emotive chord with his followers, who feel aggrieved at the decentering of white masculinity. In addition to charting the defining characteristics of Trump's discourse, *The Twitter Presidency* exposes how Trump's rhetorical style threatens democratic norms, principles, and institutions.

**Brian L. Ott** is Professor of Communication Studies and Director of the TTU Press at Texas Tech University, USA.

**Greg Dickinson** is Professor and Chair of Communication at Colorado State University, USA.

# NCA Focus on Communication Studies

NATIONAL
COMMUNICATION
ASSOCIATION

The Twitter Presidency
Donald J. Trump and the Politics of White Rage
*Brian L. Ott & Greg Dickinson*

# The Twitter Presidency

## Donald J. Trump and the Politics of White Rage

**Brian L. Ott and Greg Dickinson**

Routledge
Taylor & Francis Group

NEW YORK AND LONDON

First published 2019
by Routledge
52 Vanderbilt Avenue, New York, NY 10017

and by Routledge
2 Park Square, Milton Park, Abingdon, Oxon OX14 4RN

First issued in paperback 2020

*Routledge is an imprint of the Taylor & Francis Group, an informa
business*

© 2019 Taylor & Francis

The right of Brian L. Ott and Greg Dickinson to be identified as
authors of this work has been asserted by them in accordance with sections
77 and 78 of the Copyright, Designs and Patents Act 1988.

All rights reserved. No part of this book may be reprinted or
reproduced or utilized in any form or by any electronic, mechanical,
or other means, now known or hereafter invented, including photocopying
and recording, or in any information storage or
retrieval system, without permission in writing from the publishers.

*Trademark notice:* Product or corporate names may be trademarks
or registered trademarks, and are used only for identification and
explanation without intent to infringe.

*Library of Congress Cataloging in Publication Data*
A catalog record has been requested for this book

ISBN 13: 978-0-367-67028-3 (pbk)
ISBN 13: 978-0-367-14975-8 (hbk)

Typeset in Sabon
by Apex CoVantage, LLC

MIX
Paper from
responsible sources
FSC   FSC™ C013985
www.fsc.org

Printed in the United Kingdom
by Henry Ling Limited

# Contents

# Tables

# Reclaiming Freedom in Education

*Reclaiming Freedom in Education* examines the notion of 'freedom' within educational settings. Following an investigation of the new 'Free Schools' in the UK, it argues that this name is a misnomer, and instead explores the original free schools of the 1960s and 1970s, using these models as a lens through which to explore contemporary examples of radical schooling, notably those which describe themselves as democratic and/or progressive.

By arguing that in radical educational contexts both 'positive freedom' and 'negative freedom' are apparent, and that the notion that 'responsible freedom' is more pertinent than that of 'absolute freedom', this book posits that freedom can be seen to operate in a number of ways including 'freedom to be', 'freedom to think', 'freedom to choose' and 'freedom to self-govern'. The book:

- Describes how freedom can be used to inform educational structures, policies, pedagogies and practices across a range of settings
- Features illustrative case studies of radical free schools and alternative education spaces which have been underpinned by a commitment to freedom and to advancing social justice
- Critiques the current policy agenda to use 'freedom' to make education more competitive through claims that it correlates with higher test scores and academic success
- Considers some of the challenges for teachers, educators and students of offering and experiencing freedom in education, and argues that despite these, the case for advancing freedom is both urgent and compelling

Creating discussions about the new meaning and role that 'freedom' can have in improving education, *Reclaiming Freedom in Education* is a practical contribution to educational activism, which will be a key point of reference for teachers, parents, researchers and students on undergraduate and postgraduate courses in Education Studies, Early Childhood Studies and doctorates.

**Max A. Hope** works part-time at the University of Hull and part-time as an independent academic, educator and activist. Her key areas of interest are about radical, democratic and student-led education. She is passionate about developing more inclusive and equitable educational systems that meet the needs of all children and young people. She is co-founder of the Freedom to Learn Project (www.freedomtolearnproject.com), an international project that explores whether alternative and radical education can contribute towards social justice. She is convener of the Alternative Education Special Interest Group for the British Educational Research Association. She is a Trustee at The Warren (Hull, UK) and at Phoenix Education Trust (London, UK).

**Routledge Focus on Education Studies**
Series Editor
Will Curtis
*Academic Director (Partnerships), University of Warwick, UK*

For more information about this series: https://www.routledge.com/
Routledge-Focus-on-Education-Studies/book-series/FOCUSEDU

# Reclaiming Freedom in Education

Theories and Practices of Radical Free School Education

Max A. Hope

Routledge
Taylor & Francis Group

LONDON AND NEW YORK

First published 2019
by Routledge

2 Park Square, Milton Park, Abingdon, Oxfordshire OX14 4RN
52 Vanderbilt Avenue, New York, NY 10017

*Routledge is an imprint of the Taylor & Francis Group, an informa business*

First issued in paperback 2020

Copyright © 2019 Max A. Hope

The right of Max A. Hope to be identified as author of this work
has been asserted by her in accordance with sections 77 and 78 of
the Copyright, Designs and Patents Act 1988.

All rights reserved. No part of this book may be reprinted or reproduced or
utilised in any form or by any electronic, mechanical, or other means, now
known or hereafter invented, including photocopying and recording, or in
any information storage or retrieval system, without permission in writing
from the publishers.

Notice:
Product or corporate names may be trademarks or registered trademarks,
and are used only for identification and explanation without intent to
infringe.

*British Library Cataloguing-in-Publication Data*
A catalogue record for this book is available from the British Library

*Library of Congress Cataloging-in-Publication Data*
Names: Hope, Max (Max A.), author.
Title: Reclaiming freedom in education / Max Hope.
Description: Abingdon, Oxon ; New York, NY : Routledge, 2019. |
    Includes bibliographical references.
Identifiers: LCCN 2018038826 | ISBN 9781138048751 (hardback) |
    ISBN 9781315169972 (ebook)
Subjects: LCSH: Free schools. | Free schools—Great Britain. |
    Democracy and education—Great Britain.
Classification: LCC LB1029.F7 H64 2019 | DDC 371.04—dc23
LC record available at https://lccn.loc.gov/2018038826

ISBN: 978-1-138-04875-1 (hbk)
ISBN: 978-0-367-61638-0 (pbk)

Typeset in Times New Roman
by Apex CoVantage, LLC

MIX
Paper from
responsible sources
FSC
www.fsc.org   FSC™ C013985

Printed in the United Kingdom
by Henry Ling Limited

This book is for all the children and young people who deserved more than our education systems were able to give.

# Contents

# Table

# Acknowledgements

I have developed my enthusiasm, ideas and arguments about freedom in education over many years. My initiation into this world came through being a youth and community worker at The Warren in Hull where I met hundreds of young people who had felt restricted and constrained by negative experiences at school. Through working with them in more informal ways, I learned about the transformational nature of learning experiences that were based on freedom, trust, equality and respect. These young people, and the staff at The Warren, continue to inspire me.

As a university academic, I have been privileged to co-found the Freedom to Learn Project. This international research project was established in 2013 and has brought together many practitioners, academics, students, parents, trade unionists, teachers and school leaders. Our broad aims are to explore whether radical, democratic and alternative forms of education have the capacity to address educational inequalities and social injustice. Through this project, we have found many inspiring individuals across a range of settings – schools, colleges, universities, youth and community work, informal settings, charities – who share our commitment to developing autonomous, student-led and liberating education. Many of the ideas in this book grew out of discussions and collaborations within the Freedom to Learn Project, particularly those connected with the creation of the Freedom to Learn Manifesto.

I am profoundly grateful to everyone who has participated in the four research projects that underpin this book. These took place at Sands School (Devon, UK), Hellerup School (Copenhagen, Denmark), Pride School Atlanta (Georgia, US) and at the International Democratic Education Conference (IDEC) in Finland, 2016. I would also like to thank all the schools and other learning environments that I have been fortunate enough to visit over the last 10 years, including those in Australia, Canada, Denmark, Mexico, Portugal, Spain, the UK and the US. I have changed the names of all children, young people, teachers, parents and school leaders. The real names of case study schools have been used; those that I have visited have given permission for this, and others have been included which have previously been explicitly named in published books, newspaper articles and websites. I have presented these case studies to illustrate the arguments of this book, and some of these amalgamate data from several children and young people and combine them into composites. I have done this to protect the anonymity of individuals.

Finally, I pay tribute to Carl Rogers, person-centred psychotherapist and author of *Freedom to Learn* (1969). His work has radically altered my professional practice and opened up a new world.

# Preface

This book is making the case that in education, the notion of 'freedom' needs to be reclaimed from those in the UK and around the world who have, in recent years, used it as a tool for bringing a greater degree of competition and choice into the 'educational marketplace'. Free Schools in the UK, along with Charter Schools in the US and Free Schools in Sweden, have been heralded as new models for driving up standards in education, 'standards' which are usually equated with improved test scores and greater conformity in terms of discipline and behaviour. These people – politicians and policy-makers – have tried to distort the notion of freedom from being a radical political position that enables the human spirit to thrive and flourish, and change it into an instrumental tool for steering schools in the direction that they, the political elite, want them to go. As a result, our understanding of freedom has become more confused, and there is a struggle for meaning, particularly in terms of who is perceived as being free and what they are seen as being free from. In this context, many of the original liberation-based versions of free schools have chosen to distance themselves from the concept. This book attempts to reclaim the notion of freedom from those who have appropriated it, and to re-position it as a radical and progressive notion that schools can use to inform their structures, policies, pedagogies, processes and practices. In particular, this book is about ensuring that children and young people can have as much freedom as is practically feasible, and working through some of the challenges of doing so.

In 1850, Henry David Thoreau wrote: 'What does education often do? It makes a straight-cut ditch of a free, meandering brook' (Thoreau 2009, p. 42). Children and young people are unique, creative, wise and full of curiosity and wonder. Enabling such individuals to be themselves, to find themselves, to reach their potential and to learn what they need to learn requires teachers and facilitators to step outside of their usual frames of references and see education in a different way. It demands that adults are prepared to build alliances and partnerships with children and young people so that they can co-create the conditions for learning. It necessitates a re-imagining of schooling and of the way that schools operate.

This book is making a radical political statement. It is arguing that children and young people can be trusted and that they should be trusted. It claims that they can be responsible, that they can make good decisions, that they can be constructive members of communities. It is grounded in the conviction that children and young people want to learn and that, when given a choice, they will usually choose to learn. It is arguing that children and young people should be given more freedom, and that although this gives them power and that with 'great power there is great responsibility' (Churchill, in Parliament 1906, p. DCCCXL), they are able to embrace this responsibility.

This book is about freedom, or more precisely, about radical schools and alternative learning spaces that are underpinned by principles and practices of freedom. Described in this book as 'radical free schools', they are not to be confused with newer models of 'Free School' that have sprung up over England and Wales since 2010. Rather, the 'original' free schools of the 1960s and 1970s were progressive, democratic, community-based schools that aimed to be fundamentally different from traditional schooling and to provide free, open, liberating spaces for students. Although most of these in the UK have closed, they have parallels with many democratic, progressive and alternative schools that continue to thrive throughout the world. By re-examining the original free schools and using them as a prism through which to explore the radical free schools that exist today, this book takes a new look at the interconnected notions of freedom and social justice and argues that the case for educational institutions to offer both is urgent and compelling.

By inference, this book is sending out a challenge to parents, individual teachers, schools, and the education system as a whole, to reconsider the way they perceive the competences of children and young people. This book is aiming to be positive and to bring some optimism to practitioners, parents, students and academics who have a desire for schooling to change. Although it is important to acknowledge the flaws in the system, it is also vital to recognise that some innovative and radical schools are going against the grain. These stories are helpful in acting as catalysts for new discussions to take place. As Dewey argued, 'If we want individuals to be free we must see to it that suitable conditions exist: a truism which at least indicates the direction in which to look and move' (Dewey 1940, p. 34). By sharing stories of schools which manage to work against the tidal wave of neoliberalism and do something alternative, this book aims to indicate the direction in which teachers and schools might want to look and move.

This book strives to offer a sense of hope that education can change, not just in the interests of some children and young people, but for all. It is underpinned, of course, by a damning critique of neoliberalism and of the way that conventional schooling is currently structured in the UK and elsewhere. It argues, through using case examples and stories of radical and progressive practices, that there is another way – a better way – of educating children and young people.

This is not just a theoretical book. It strives to make a contribution to educational activism. It is embedded in pedagogy and practice. It is sharing stories of schools and alternative learning spaces that do things differently – stories which have the power to inspire others to view the world differently. It is an invitation to see education in a new light, a plea to step out of familiar frames of references and take some risks. It is a call to action.

## References

Dewey, J. 1940. *Freedom and Culture*. London: Kimble and Bradford.
Parliament, Great Britain. 1906. *The Parliamentary Debates*. London: Reuter's Telegram Company.
Thoreau, H.D. 2009. *The Journal of Henry David Thoreau, 1837–1861*. New York: New York Review Books Classics.

# 1 Introduction
## The notion of 'freedom'

### Introduction

'Freedom' is a word we use badly and strangely.

(Holt 1972, p. 15)

What does 'freedom' mean and what does it look like when introduced to schools, in terms of its implications for staff, students, parents and the wider community? Why is freedom an important concept within education? What benefits – or pitfalls – might it bring? These questions are all important to address in a book which explores freedom in education, or as the title of this book suggests, *reclaims* freedom in education.

When Carl Rogers wrote his seminal text *Freedom to Learn* in 1969, he challenged dominant discourses about education, schooling, how children learn and how teachers teach. He did not, however, provide a strong definition of what he meant by 'freedom'. There is an assumption in his work, and in the work of many other scholars, that the meaning of this word is clear and undisputed. This is not the case. In recent years, 'freedom' has been heralded both as a panacea which will help to save the failing education system (Gove 2010, 13 May 2011; Cameron 8 July 2010) and as a dangerous trend which threatens to radicalise children (Williams 9 June 2015; Santry 20 October 2016). This book takes a different stance from both of these views.

Freedom is a complex and contested concept. The language associated with freedom – such as autonomy, liberty, choice, self-determination, democracy – can be used in contrasting ways to promote particular agendas. There is therefore a need for more theoretical work on the nature of freedom in education, and this book is striving to go some way toward addressing this need. Although it is not primarily a theoretical book, this first chapter delves into some of the debates about the nature of freedom and tries to create a clear and useful definition for what freedom in education might mean.

In addition, it starts to make the case, further developed throughout this book, that a commitment to freedom should be inseparable from the desire to tackle inequalities and advance social justice.

This chapter attempts to untangle some of the complex debates about freedom and social justice, and in turn, to present clear notions as to how both are characterised within this book. This process has been vastly aided through conversations with colleagues in the Freedom to Learn Project, through which a manifesto was created which attempted to summarise what educational organisations which value a 'freedom to learn' might need to consider (see Montgomery and Hope 2016; Freedom to Learn Project 2017). Although this book does not use the same formulation as that used in the Freedom to Learn Manifesto, there are similarities with the approach taken in terms of distinguishing between negative freedom (freedom from), positive freedom (freedom to) and real freedom (agency) (Berlin 1969/2007; Van Parijs 1995/2007). The notions of absolute freedom and responsible or negotiated freedom are also clarified in this chapter. The relationship between freedom and social justice is explored, especially in the light of claims that the new 'freedoms' offered to post-2010 Free Schools enable them to be 'engines of social justice' (Bloom 22 May 2015).

The central focus of this book is on sharing stories of innovative and radical practices that illustrate the theoretical arguments contained within this chapter. Details about these case studies and stories, the data that underpin them and the way they are used are outlined towards the end of this chapter.

## Why is freedom important to explore?: current political context

Improving education systems and educational outcomes has been a major area of concern for numerous governments for many decades. Across the western and non-western world, political parties have been known to stand or fall depending on their record on education. International league tables, compiled through Program for International Student Assessment (PISA) statistics, rank countries against one another and compel governments to pay attention to policies, practices and teaching standards in other countries (OECD 2013). The political climate of neoliberalism is central to this. Neoliberal economies have gathered momentum in the last 30 years, with the underpinning philosophy that the 'market saves', that the market can improve standards through bringing competition and choice to a consumer-driven marketplace (Ball 2008; Reay 2012; Monbiot 2017). Within this climate, an international focus on freedom – and indeed, social justice – has become pronounced, with countries such as the UK, Czech Republic, the Netherlands, Sweden, Finland, Macao-China, the US and

Australia all claiming that increased autonomy correlates with improved standards (OECD 2004, 2011). Far-reaching and seemingly non-reversible policies have emanated from this position, resulting in the establishment of hundreds of new Free Schools, Charter Schools and Academies. These are underpinned by a philosophy, exemplified by Michael Gove, former Secretary of State for Education in England, who argued that 'by freeing school leaders from bureaucracy . . . we give them more space to innovate, to excel, and by excelling, to inspire others' (Gove 2010). It is imperative to note, nonetheless, that within this discourse, freedom and autonomy are offered to *schools* and *school leaders* but not usually to *students* (McGregor 2009; Gerrard 2014). Freedom, here, is for adults. They are freed from the control of external authorities and subsequently, become freer to innovate. By way of contrast, within many of these new 'free' schools, students experience greater levels of regulation, narrower curricula and stricter discipline (Hatcher 2010; Boyask 2013).

This book explores the nature of freedom within a markedly different type of educational establishment, described here as 'radical free schools'. In particular, it focuses on the notion of 'freedom to learn', a term explicitly used by Rogers (Rogers 1969, 1980; Rogers and Freiberg 1994) and cohering with arguments presented by Apple (Apple 2000; Apple and Beane 1999); Dewey (2004); Freire (1970, 1994, 2001); hooks (1994); Neill (1937, 1962). This term, though frequently used, is ambiguous and its meaning is imprecise. It relates to the freedom experienced by *students* within education, which, these authors advocate, should be greater than that usually present within conventional educational systems.

Nelson Mandela stated in 1995 that 'there can be no keener revelation of a society's soul than the way in which it treats its children' (Mandela 8 May 1995). Children and young people are rarely, if ever, seen as citizens in their own right, and there is almost a common acceptance that their rights, along with their freedom, are different from those of adults. There are many assumptions about the competence of children and young people to be trusted, to be responsible, to make their own decisions, and as a result, adults usually step in and make decisions on their behalf. The education of children and young people is no exception. Adults invariably make most decisions on the curriculum, the pedagogy, the assessment strategy, and even the seating plans and the grouping arrangements. Children are rarely genuinely involved in making significant decisions (Hart 1992). They are occasionally consulted – at best – but usually not even that. The situation is even worse for younger children, with some scholars and practitioners arguing that young children are not competent to be involved in making decisions on any level.

The notion of freedom grounding the arguments in this book is the one relating to enhancing freedom for *students*. Freedom, here, is for children, young people *and* adults. It is thus quite different from the notion of freedom that is most frequently promoted by neoliberal politicians. In their capacity as students and as human beings, children, young people and adults are freed from constraining structures and processes and are thus able to experience a greater degree of autonomy and self-determination.

## Brief history of free schools: 'original free schools' and 'post-2010 Free Schools'

In the UK, 'Free Schools' were created as part of the Academies Act 2010, and since this point, nearly 500 new Free Schools have opened in the primary, secondary, alternative provision and special education sectors (Department for Education 2017). The model was loosely based on Swedish Free Schools and on Charter Schools in the US, both of which were extensively referenced at the time as being models to emulate. Charter Schools were described as 'the quintessential model of school autonomy', which 'are helping these pupils achieve amazing things'. In Sweden, it was claimed that 'pupils at these schools get better results than pupils at traditional schools; that Free Schools improve standards across the local authority; and that parental satisfaction has significantly increased' (Gove 20 June 2011).

Free Schools, nonetheless, are not a new invention. Summerhill School in Suffolk opened in 1921 and describes itself as 'the original, alternative "free" school' (Summerhill School 2017). There were also 14 state-funded 'free schools' in England and Scotland in the 1960s and 1970s. These were quite different from the 21st-century versions. These 'original free schools' served working-class communities and were universally perceived as progressive (de Castella 21 October 2014). They were community-based 'schools without walls', unrestricted by rigid curricula, school hours or term dates. Each one was different in terms of how it was structured and what it offered, but all shared similar ambitions to be radically different from traditional schooling and to provide free, open spaces that were liberated from conventional hierarchies and disciplinary structures.

The development of these schools in the UK was part of a worldwide movement towards progressive education. In the US, the 1960s and 1970s witnessed the emergence of hundreds of free schools across a variety of states, several of which still exist in their original format. Most notable of these were Sudbury Valley School, MA (est. 1968) (Sudbury Valley School 2017) and Albany Free School, NY (est. 1969) (Albany Free School 2017), both of which have been credited with influencing the development of democratic, progressive and/or radical education across the world. Although many of the early free schools closed down in the US, the free school model continues to thrive in the US, with many new schools being established every year. One of these discussed in detail in this book is Pride School Atlanta (est. 2016), a new democratic free school which, by describing itself as 'LGBTQ[1]-affirming', additionally demonstrates a radical commitment to social justice (Pride School Atlanta 2017). This school has parallels with the 'Freedom Schools' in Mississippi (est. 1964), which are interesting illustrations of schools which are explicitly designed to challenge traditional curricula and pedagogies and advance social justice (Hale 2011). These schools will be explored in more detail in Chapter Four.

This book investigates, mainly in Chapter Two, the rise and fall of the original free schools in the UK, largely focussing on the example of White Lion Free School, London and Scotland Road Free School, Liverpool. These schools experienced many problems and eventually closed, along with all 14 original free schools in the UK. They are not presented here in an idealised or uncritical manner; rather, they are offered as useful prisms through which to view the complex issues and challenges that come with attempting to offer freedom to students. Through exploring these issues, and the history of the free school movement in the US, it becomes apparent that these free schools bear little resemblance to the new incarnations of 'Free School' which, though free from local authority governance, exhibit many institutional practices which are premised on traditional hierarchical and authoritarian relationships and notions of knowledge.

Through investigating the original free schools, several central issues emerge that need to be considered and effectively addressed within radical free schools. These challenges are not those that face contemporary Free Schools as they do not share the same aims and aspirations of the original free schools; in fact, it is argued that using the word 'free' is a misnomer when applied to the newer versions. For that reason, it is more useful to compare the original Free Schools in the UK with democratic, progressive and/or radical schools in the UK and beyond. Nonetheless, it is crucial to include analysis of the newer versions so as to ensure that readers are able to make the distinction between schools which use the same descriptor. This forms the focus of Chapter Two.

## Theoretical underpinnings: freedom and social justice

The precise definition of the term 'freedom' is ambiguous and has been debated for centuries (Gray 1991). Over the past few hundred years, though, and even further back into history, the common discourse around freedom is that it is, in essence, a good thing. The Founding Documents of the US, created over 200 years ago, are known collectively as the 'Charters of Freedom' and specify many liberties and rights which are guaranteed to this day (see National Archives 2017). The Magna Carta (1215) – the 'Great Charter of the Liberties of England' – established the notion of freedom under the law (see British Library 2017). The Universal Declaration of Human Rights (United Nations 1948) states that 'All human beings are born free and equal in dignity and rights'. Despite these charters and laws, it is widely accepted that freedom is *not* universally available to all humans, and consequently, the aspiration that 'all men [people] are created equal' (as stated in the US Declaration of Independence) has never been fully realised. Social inequalities and social injustice has meant that freedom, like rights, seems to be more available to some people than to others. Tying a commitment to freedom with an agenda for advancing social justice is thus essential. Freedom for some should not be at the detriment of freedom for others. This coheres with Macmurray's (1949, p. 74) eloquent proposition that 'any attempt to achieve freedom without equality, or to achieve equality without freedom, must, therefore, be self-defeating'.

Neoliberal governments around the world have drawn on the discourse of freedom to justify their education policies, such as those establishing Free Schools, Charter Schools and Academies. Significantly, they have also been driven by arguments about social mobility and social justice. In the UK, for example, the Conservative Party has frequently made explicit links between Free Schools and their role in improving social mobility and reducing social inequalities. Nicky Morgan, Education Secretary (2014–2016), described them as the 'modern engines of social justice' (Bloom 22 May 2015). It appears that through using their freedom to innovate, these new models of schooling have been perceived as having the power to address deep-seated issues of social inequality in the UK. The credibility of these claims will be explored in Chapter Two.

When used by politicians and policy-makers, the concept of 'social justice' is frequently conflated with 'social mobility'. This reduces the debate to one about *school admissions* and *academic attainment* in relation to children of different *socio-economic backgrounds*. This notion of social justice coheres with arguments about the importance of redistribution of resources (Fraser 1998). Although crucial, this interpretation is narrow and does not address wider concerns about cultural recognition and about the need to respect diverse identities and offer love, care and solidarity (Fraser 1998; Lynch and Baker 2005). Some schools strive to do both. The Freedom Schools in the US, for example, had an explicit agenda to address social injustice. These originated in 1964 as a summer project to offer a radical culture of resistance, with a curriculum and associated pedagogy which was designed to challenge the dominant assumptions and prejudices which were built into the fabric of conventional education (Hale 2011; Jackson and Howard 2014). In Chapter Four of this book, an examination of these schools, as well as other more contemporary cases, provide compelling stories of schools that offer freedom as well as maintaining a powerful commitment to tackling inequalities and advancing social justice. They are reflective of the notion of social justice that underpins this book. This mirrors Fraser's (1998, p. 1, emphasis in original) argument that 'Justice today requires *both* redistribution *and* recognition. Neither alone is sufficient'.

In an endeavour to define freedom as precisely as possible, it makes sense to turn first to Berlin's 'Two Concepts of Liberty' (Berlin 1969/2007), one of the most prominent contributions to this field. Berlin delineates freedom into two categories: as *negative freedom* (freedom from external constraint) and as *positive freedom* (freedom to self-determine one's own life). He described negative freedom as a lack of interference or coercion:

> I am normally said to be free to the degree which no man or body of men interferes with my activity. . . . If I am prevented by others from doing what I could otherwise do, I am to that degree unfree; and if this area is contracted by other men beyond a certain minimum, I can be described as being coerced, or, it may be, enslaved.
>
> (Berlin 1969/2007, p. 39)

Positive freedom, on the other hand, is intertwined with autonomy and self-will. It is where

> I wish my life and decisions to depend on myself, not on external forces of whatever kind. . . . I wish to be a subject, not an object; to be moved by reasons, by conscious purposes, which are my own, not by causes which affect me, as it were, from outside.
>
> (Berlin 1969/2007, p. 44)

Van Parijs (1995/2007) has added the conception of *real freedom* to these two, arguing that freedom can only be realised in practice if an individual has the power – the 'opportunity' – to take advantage of both positive and negative freedom. *Agency* might be another word for opportunity. Agency, described by Macmurray (1949, p. 49) as 'the means of action', is a vital element for the enactment of freedom in educational settings. Without agency, both positive and negative freedom remain largely notional.

Berlin's (1969/2007) model of negative and positive freedom, though widely adopted, has been criticised for its binary nature. Gray (1991, p. 9) argues that 'these labels are quite unhelpful, since virtually any kind of liberty could be expressed in terms of either "freedom from" *or* "freedom to" . . . '. In the context of education, this argument has merit. Issues of freedom, autonomy and agency are complex and open to interpretation.

It is not possible to make entirely neutral judgments as to what constitute negative and positive freedom; these are partially context and child-specific. As some of the stories in this book show, a constraint for one child might be liberating for another. Nonetheless, exploring freedom in terms of negative, positive and real freedom is a useful starting point, and thus, these three interrelated concepts are central to the formulation of freedom that is employed within this book. These are used as a lens through which to view freedom for students and freedom for schools. They are a powerful way of exploring who has freedom and what this freedom enables them to be 'free from. . . ' and 'free to. . . '.

Chapter Two examines the new models of Free Schools that have been developed post-2010 and compares these with the original free schools of the 1960s and 1970s. It will use the notions of 'freedom from' and 'freedom to' as tools to compare the types of freedom which each of these models exhibit. Chapters Three and Four will use stories and case studies to explore, in depth, how radical free schools develop structures, policies, pedagogies, processes and practices which enable them to offer real 'freedom from. . . ' and 'freedom to. . . ' students. This book argues that offering freedom is not a categorical issue in that educational establishments either *do* or *do not* offer freedom; this would fit with the notion of absolute freedom, which this book claims is unhelpful. Rather, radical free schools are seen as those which offer *a level* of responsible freedom to students, a negotiated concept which necessitates that students are accountable for the impact of their actions, and work within constraints and boundaries. As can be seen from the case studies and stories offered within this book, the level of this 'responsible freedom' might depend, in part, on the age of the child in question (Bessant 2014). Freedom in schools will be considered on both a micro level and a macro level, recognising that freedom might take many forms, including that relating to the individual (micro) or to the whole-school level (macro) (Morrison 2008).

Some of the early definitions of freedom posit that any constraints upon freedom means that an individual is unfree or enslaved. Mill (1859, p. 72), for example, argued that 'The only freedom that deserves the name is that of pursuing our own good in our own way'. This definition alludes to the state of having *absolute freedom*; that is, where an individual is able to do whatever they want; that they are 'free from' everything and 'free to' do anything. This extreme form of freedom is seldom available to individuals who live in any degree of contact with others. Arguably, it is so rare as to be significant only as a theoretical proposition and not as a practical reality. In addition, it is unusual to hear arguments that individuals should have absolute and unfettered freedom in schools, even if it were theoretically possible. Few would argue, for example, that students should have the freedom to bear arms or the right to act in ways that cause intolerable levels of offence to others. There are limits to freedom, and thus, offering absolute freedom in schools is entirely undesirable. Even schools which claim to offer freedom to students, such as Summerhill School in the UK and Sudbury Schools in the US, categorically deny that they offer absolute freedom (Neill 1962; Skogen 2010). A.S. Neill, founder of Summerhill School, for example, stated that: 'Freedom means doing what you like, *so long as you don't interfere with the freedom of others*' (Neill 1962, p. 114, emphasis added). He explains that:

> There isn't such a thing as absolute freedom. Anyone who allows a child to get his own way is following a dangerous path. No-one can have social freedom, for the rights of others must be respected. But everyone should have individual freedom.
>
> (Neill 1962, p. 309)

Neill frequently draws the distinction between 'freedom' and 'license' (Neill 1962). This indicates that freedom is, to some extent, a negotiated concept. This resonates with theories of autonomy in sociological thought, and in particular, the concept of 'relative autonomy' (Fritzell 1987; Gordon 1989; Apple 2002). This is reinforced by empirical data from teachers, parents and students in radical free schools across the world. Lee, a 17-year-old student in Hong Kong, emphatically stated that 'I don't think there is absolute freedom in democratic education'. Emilie, an educator from Brazil, argued that 'for me freedom is to do what you believe and what you are passionate about without hurting anyone and anything'. For Sapna, a teacher from India, freedom means that 'you keep your duties in mind *and* exercise your rights' (IDEC Group Interview 2016).

Rogers (1980, p. 305) uses the phrase 'responsible freedom' to refer to the type of freedom offered within educational institutions. In *Freedom to Learn* (1969), he is unequivocal in his defence of offering responsible – as opposed to absolute – freedom:

> Children as well as adults can accept reasonable requirements which are placed on them by society or by the institution. The point is that when freedom and self-direction are given to a group, it is also easier for the members to accept the constraints and obligations which surround the psychological area in which they are free.
>
> (Rogers 1969, p. 24)

This distinction between absolute and responsible freedom, or between freedom and license, is crucial to understand, and is a central element of the formulation of 'freedom' that grounds this book. Freedom is not absolute. Responsible freedom requires negotiation with others who might be impacted by one's actions, and so offering this type of freedom in schools demands a level of engagement and interaction with others. Macmurray (1949, p. 25) made this case when he argued that 'our freedom, as individuals, depends on the co-operation of others. We are fed and clothed by our fellows. The whole apparatus of our life is provided by others'. This, according to Säfström and Biesta (2011, p. 540), means that 'freedom is relational and therefore inherently difficult'. Freedom brings with it a set of responsibilities.

There is key question to address, nonetheless, and this relates to whether all people – children, young people and adults – have equal entitlement to responsible or negotiated freedom. The central issue is whether everyone has the capacity to take the necessary level of responsibility.

Critics argue, for example, that children in primary school are simply too young to be trusted with making choices about their learning, that young people will make poor choices if they are not strongly directed towards good ones, that university students do not have the capacity to know what it best for them (Arendt 1961; Peal 2014; Furedi 2010). The restriction of freedom, therefore, is justified on the grounds that someone else (parents, teachers, institutions, governments) is better placed to use it. Freedom, where it exists, is limited to making choices between an extremely narrow set of alternatives. This, according to Gray (1991), does not constitute freedom in any meaningful sense. The question of whether children and young people are competent and thus able to use freedom is crucial to address in the context of schooling. This will be addressed throughout this book, principally in relation to questions of age (see, in particular, Chapter Five).

Within radical free schools, students and staff have to be able to communicate together, as equals, and they have to be willing to acknowledge that everyone shares a right to freedom. Although there might be some differences that relate to the ages of students, every school member has the right to experience and use freedom. Clearly, this significantly changes the role of teachers (adults) within radical free schools. It does not mean they have to be passive, but it does change the nature of the student-teacher relationship. Rogers (1969, 1980) argues that their role is as 'facilitators', and Freire (1970, p. 74) describes them as 'teacher-student with student-teachers'. Säfström and Biesta (2011, p. 540, emphasis added) posit that 'educational freedom is not about the absence of authority but about *authority that carries an orientation towards freedom* with it'. Saulius, a parent from Lithuania, echoed this by explaining that 'anyone becomes a learner and anyone becomes a teacher' (IDEC Group Interview 2016). In order to fulfil these roles effectively, it is essential that teachers (or educators, facilitators) inhabit a particular set of values about the nature of freedom, the value of freedom and the capabilities of children and young people. These values will be explored in more depth throughout this book, and the implications of this will be addressed in detail in the final chapter.

## Brief summary of illustrative cases used in this book

This book is grounded in published academic literature from the fields of philosophy, sociology and education, which is used to examine the precise nature of freedom and its applicability to educational contexts. It draws extensively on books, memoirs and archive material from those directly involved in radical free schools, both from the 1960s and 1970s and from the present day (including Hecht 2011; Greenberg 1987; Wright 1989; Neill 1962). None of these are heralded as 'ideal' or 'perfect' examples of schools which offer freedom to students; rather, they are all presented as interesting cases to illustrate the arguments of this book.

In addition, this book uses original empirical data, by way of observations and direct quotations, which are woven throughout the book. These come from four main sources. The first three of these consist of data from the author's previous studies which have been re-analysed through the specific lens of 'freedom'. These were from a grounded theory study about students' experiences of democratic education in the UK (Hope 2010), from qualitative case studies of an innovative Danish school and a radical Danish university (Hope and Montgomery 2016), and from a place-based case study of a new LGBTQ-affirming free school in Atlanta (Hope and Hall 2018; Hall and Hope 2018). Some of these data have been creatively re-written as 'case studies' or 'composite stories' to illustrate the experiences of students and the practices of radical free schools. These are presented in Chapters Three and Four. Fourth, new data were gathered, by the author, through a large group interview with 21 teachers, students and parents from 13 countries. This took place at the International Democratic Education Conference (IDEC) in Finland in June 2016. This semi-structured group interview included participants from Australia, Brazil, Canada, France, Germany, India, Hong Kong, Lithuania, Poland, Taiwan, UK and US. This interview focussed on two main research questions: 1) What language do staff, parents and students within radical free schools use when discussing 'freedom'; and 2) How do staff, parents and students describe their experiences of 'freedom' within radical free schools? Quotations from this interview are weaved throughout this book (cited as IDEC Group Interview 2016). All names are pseudonyms.

The democratic, progressive and/or radical schools and alternative learning spaces that feature most heavily in this book are outlined in Table 1.1. Further details will be given throughout the book.

Table 1.1 Information on illustrative case studies

| Name | Location | Date Established | Approx number of students | Age range |
|---|---|---|---|---|
| White Lion Free School | London, UK | 1972 (closed 1990) | 50 (max) | secondary |
| Scotland Road Free School | Liverpool, UK | 1971 (closed 1975) | 50 (max) | secondary |
| Sands School | Devon, UK | 1987 | 70 | 11–17 |
| Summerhill School | Suffolk, UK | 1921 | 70 | 5–18 |
| Hellerup School | Copenhagen, Denmark | 2002 | 660 | 6–16 |
| Sudbury Valley School | Massachusetts, US | 1968 | 140 | 4–19 |
| Democratic School of Hadera | Hadera, Israel | 1987 | 650 | 4–18 |
| Pride School Atlanta | Atlanta, US | 2016 | 12 | 5–18 |
| Mississippi Freedom Schools | Mississippi, US | 1964 | 2000-2500 across 41 schools | All ages |
| CDF Freedom Schools | Various, US | 1995 | 137,000 across 30 states | 4–19 |
| Black Supplementary Schools | Various, UK | 1960s | 50 schools | various |
| Free We Grow | London, UK | 2017 | 12 | 5–11 |

## Structure of this book

Chapter Two sets the scene by looking at the nature of some of the original free schools of the 1960s and 1970s so as to provide a historical context for this book. These free schools had an agenda, not just to advance freedom but to enhance social justice. They were set up to meet the needs of some of the most disadvantaged and excluded children and young people, many of whom were living in extreme poverty and for whom schooling was not seen as a priority. These schools are of great significance when it comes to exploring the nature of freedom in education, because although they all eventually closed down, they were genuinely radical social experiments, from which many of the lessons have not yet been fully explored. They are useful to us to consider today, especially when used as a prism through which to view the newer post-2010 'Free Schools', which as Chapter Two will argue, is a misnomer.

Chapter Three brings case study examples of radical schools that use freedom in interesting ways. These examples are used to illustrate the theoretical case, made in this chapter, about how freedom might be conceptualised, in terms of 'freedom from', 'freedom to', 'real freedom', 'responsible freedom', and micro and macro levels of freedom. This chapter contains a significant quantity of data to illustrate the case, written in the format of stories. These centre on two main cases: Sands School (UK) and Hellerup School (Denmark), with additional material from Summerhill School (UK), Sudbury Valley School (US) and Democratic School of Hadera (Israel).

Chapter Four makes the argument that freedom needs to be allied with a commitment to advancing social justice. Radical examples of education, including Mississippi Freedom Schools (US), CDF Freedom Schools (US), Black Supplementary Schools (UK) and Pride School Atlanta (US), are offered as cases which have held a dual commitment to freedom and to social justice.

Chapter Five is slightly different from the rest of the book in that it has a specific focus on one aspect of radical free schools, that of 'freedom to choose' and how decisions are made in self-governing communities. Different methods are explored and an argument presented about some of the central characteristics that might be necessary to ensure effective self-governance within radical free schools. Examples from Summerhill School and Free We Grow are included here.

The final chapter (Chapter Six) is a position statement and makes the case for why giving greater freedom to students is both urgent and compelling. It presents arguments as to why reclaiming freedom in education is valuable and how this might take place. It considers some of the complex challenges and implications for teachers. This chapter ends with a final call to action.

## Summary

In 1972, at the height of the growing movement for opening new 'free schools' in the UK, US and beyond, Holt (1972, p. 15) wrote that ' "Freedom" is a word we use badly and strangely'. Over 40 years later, this statement is perhaps more accurate than it has ever been. 'Freedom' is a word that is increasingly associated with neoliberalism, and the concept is heralded as a panacea which can resolve many modern-day educational concerns about inequalities, 'failing' students and 'failing' schools. This is highly problematic, and it has distorted the notion of freedom. As this book argues, in this chapter and throughout, it is imperative that the notion of freedom is reclaimed and reconceptualised by those committed to radical, democratic and/or progressive education.

Freedom is a complex and contested complex, and whilst this book is not primarily theoretical, this chapter has explored several pertinent definitions and theories. In an attempt to provide conceptual clarity, the theoretical framework that grounds this book is summarised as follows:

- The discourse of freedom frequently refers to enhancing freedom for schools and school leaders. The emphasis in this book is on enhancing freedom for *students*.
- There is a necessity for freedom and social justice to be intertwined (Macmurray 1949). A commitment to enhancing freedom for some should not be at the detriment of freedom for others.
- The concept of social justice is broader than simply relating to redistribution of resources, but also involves a commitment to cultural recognition (Fraser 1998; Baker et al. 2004).
- The associated concepts of negative freedom ('freedom from'), positive freedom ('freedom to') and real freedom (agency or opportunity) will be utilised throughout this book (Berlin 1969/2007; Van Parijs 1995/2007).
- 'Absolute freedom' has been rejected as unhelpful and largely hypothetical, and the distinction is drawn between freedom and license (Neill 1962).
- The lens of 'responsible' or 'negotiated' freedom will be employed to explore the way in which 'freedom' is offered within radical free schools (Rogers 1980).
- Freedom on both micro (individual) and macro (whole-school) levels will be identified in relation to a range of case studies (Morrison 2008).

Each chapter uses stories and case studies from radical free schools across the world. Some of these stories originate from empirical data gathered by the author, and others are informed by published accounts from those working in, or attending, these schools. These case studies are not intended to act as models to emulate but as opportunities to explore how 'freedom' is enacted in practice across a variety of geographical, social and political contexts. By the final chapter, these are drawn together into a series of central themes which might be considered by all of those – teachers, students, parents, academics, school leaders – with a commitment to advancing freedom and social justice within education.

## Note

1 LGBTQ refers here to lesbian, gay, bisexual, transgendered and queer.

## References

*Albany Free School*. 2017. "Home Page." Accessed 30/11/17. Available at: www.albanyfreeschool.org/.

Apple, M.W. 2000. *Official Knowledge: Democratic Education in a Conservative Age*. New York: Routledge.

Apple, M.W. 2002. "Does Education Have Independent Power? Bernstein and the Question of Relative Autonomy." *British Journal of Sociology of Education* 23 (4):607–16.

Apple, M.W., and J.A. Beane. 1999. *Democratic Schools: Lessons from the Chalk Face*. Buckingham: Open University Press.

Arendt, H. 1961. *Six Exercises in Political Thought*. London: Faber and Faber.

Baker, J., K. Lynch, S. Cantillon, and J. Walsh. 2004. *Equality: From Theory to Action*. Hampshire: Palgrave MacMillan.

Ball, S.J. 2008. *The Education Debate*. Bristol: Policy Press.

Berlin, I. 1969/2007. "Two Concepts of Liberty (1969)." In *Freedom: A Philosophical Anthology*, edited by I. Carter, M.H. Kramer and H. Steiner. Oxford: Blackwell Publishing.

Bessant, J. 2014. "A Dangerous Idea? Freedom, Children and the Capability Approach to Education." *Critical Studies in Education* 55 (2):138–53.

Bloom, A. 22 May 2015. "Free schools are 'engines of social justice', Morgan says." In *Times Educational Supplement*.

Boyask, R. 2013. "Theorising the Democratic Potential of Privatised Schools Through the Case of Free Schools." *ACCESS: Critical Perspectives on Communication, Cultural & Policy Studies* 31 (1 and 2):11–26.

*British Library*. 2017. "Magna Carta." Accessed 30/11/17. Available at: www.bl.uk/collection-items/magna-carta-1215.

Cameron, D. 8 July 2010. "We will make government accountable to the people." In *Speech at the Civil Service Conference*, London. Available at: www.conservatives.com/News/Speeches/2010/07/David_Cameron_We_will_make_government_accountable_to_the_people.aspx.

de Castella, T. 21 October 2014. "The anarchic experimental schools of the 1970s." In *BBC News Magazine*.

Department for Education. 2017. "Free Schools: Open Schools and Successful Applications." Accessed 29/11/17. Available at: https://www.gov.uk/government/publications/free-schools-open-schools-and-successful-applications.

Dewey, J. 2004. *Democracy and Education*. New York: Dover Publications (originally published 1916).

Fraser, N. 1998. "Social justice in the age of identity politics: Redistribution, recognition, participation." In *Discussion paper // Wissenschaftszentrum Berlin für Sozialforschung, Forschungsschwerpunkt Arbeitsmarkt und Beschäftigung, Abteilung Organisation und Beschäftigung, No. FS I 98–108*.

Freedom to Learn Project. 2017. "Freedom to Learn Manifesto." Accessed 29/11/17. Available at: http://www.freedomtolearnproject.com/new/manifesto/.

Freire, P. 1970. *Pedagogy of the Oppressed*. London: Penguin Books.

Freire, P. 1994. *A Pedagogy of Hope*. London: Bloomsbury Publishing.

Freire, P. 2001. *Pedagogy of Freedom: Ethics, Democracy and Civic Courage*. Maryland: Rowman and Littlefield Publishers Inc.

Fritzell, C. 1987. "On the Concept of Relative Autonomy in Educational Theory." *British Journal of Sociology of Education* 8 (1):23–35.

Furedi, F. 2010. *Wasted: Why Education Isn't Educating*. London: Continuum Books.

Gerrard, J. 2014. "Counter-narratives of Educational Excellence: Free Schools, Success, and Community-based Schooling." *British Journal of Sociology of Education* 35 (6):876–94.

Gordon, L. 1989. "Beyond Relative Autonomy Theories of the State in Education." *British Journal of Sociology of Education* 10 (4):435–47.

Gove, M. 2010. "Speech to the association of school and college leaders." In *ASCL Annual Conference*, London. Available at: www.governmentinitiativesiq.com/michaelGoveFinal.pdf.

Gove, M. 13 May 2011. "Academies: Making partnerships work." In *Speech at Wellington Academy*, Wiltshire. Available at: www.wellingtoncollege.org.uk/conferences/earlier-conferences – /academies-making-partnerships-work – 13-may.

Gove, M. 20 June 2011. "Speech on free schools." In *Speech at The Policy Exchange*, London. Available at: www.education.gov.uk/inthenews/speeches/a0077948/michael-goves-speech-to-the-policy-exchange-on-free-schools.

Gray, T. 1991. *Freedom*. London: MacMillan Education Ltd.

Greenberg, D. 1987. *Free at Last: The Sudbury Valley School*. Massachusetts: Sudbury Valley School Press.

Hale, J.N. 2011. "The Freedom Schools, the Civil Rights Movement, and Refocusing the Goals of American Education." *The Journal of Social Studies Research* 35 (2):259–76.

Hall, J.J., and M.A. Hope. 2018. "Lost in Translation: Naming Practices and Public Feelings Towards 'Gay Schools'." In *Youth Sexualities: Public Feelings and Contemporary Cultural Politics*, edited by S. Talburt. California: Praeger.

Hart, R. 1992. *Children's Participation: From Tokenism to Citizenship, Innocenti Essays No 4*. Florence: UNICEF.

Hatcher, R. 2010. "New Lessons from England's Schools: New Forms of Privatisation and the Challenge for Local Democracy." *Our Schools/Our Selves* 19 (4):79.

Hecht, Y. 2011. *Democratic Education: A Beginning of a Story*. New York: Alternative Education Resource Organization.

Holt, J. 1972. *Freedom and Beyond*. New York: E.P. Dutton and Company Inc.

hooks, b. 1994. *Teaching to Trangress: Education as the Practice of Freedom*. Oxon: Routledge.

Hope, M.A. 2010. "Trust me, I'm a student: An exploration through Grounded Theory of the student experience in two small schools." University of Hull.

Hope, M.A., and J.J. Hall. 2018. " 'This Feels like a Whole New Thing': A Case Study of a New LGBTQ-affirming School and Its Role in Developing 'Inclusions'." *International Journal of Inclusive Education*. DOI: 10.1080/13603116.2018.1427152. Available at: www.tandfonline.com/doi/full/10.1080/13603116.2018.1427152.

Hope, M.A, and C. Montgomery. 2016. "Creating Spaces for Autonomy: The Architecture of Learning and Thinking in Danish Schools and Universities." In *The Palgrave International Handbook of Alternative Education*, edited by H. Lees and N. Noddings. Basingstoke: Palgrave Macmillan.

Jackson, T.O., and T.C. Howard. 2014. "The Continuing Legacy of Freedom Schools as Sites of Possibility for Equity and Social Justice for Black Students." *The Western Journal of Black Studies* 38 (3):155–62.

Lynch, K., and J. Baker. 2005. "Equality in Education: An Equality of Condition Perspective." *Theory and Research in Education* 3 (2):131–64.

Macmurray, J. 1949. *Conditions of Freedom*. London: Faber and Faber Ltd.

Mandela, N. 8 May 1995. "Speech by President Nelson Mandela at the launch of the Nelson Mandela Children's Fund." In *Launch of the Nelson Mandela Children's Fund*. Mahlamba Ndlopfu, Pretoria, South Africa. Available at: http://db.nelsonmandela.org/speeches/pub_view.asp?pg=item&ItemID=NMS250&txtstr=Mahla.

McGregor, G. 2009. "Educating for (Whose) Success? Schooling in an Age of Neoliberalism." *British Journal of Sociology of Education* 30 (3):345–58.

Mill, J.S. 1859. *On Liberty*. London: Penguin Books.

Monbiot, G. 2017. *Out of the Wreckage: A New Politics for an Age of Crisis*. London: Verso.

Montgomery, C., and M.A. Hope. 2016. "Thinking the Yet to Be Thought: Envisioning Autonomous and Alternative Pedagogies for Socially Just Education." *FORUM: For Promoting 3–19 Comprehensive Education*.

Morrison, K.A. 2008. "Democratic Classrooms: Promises and Challenges of Student Voice and Choice, Part One." *Educational Horizons* 87 (1):50–60.

*National Archives*. 2017. "America's Founding Documents." Accessed 30/11/17. Available at: www.archives.gov/founding-docs.

Neill, A.S. 1937. *That Dreadful School*. London: Herbert Jenkins Ltd.

Neill, A.S. 1962. *Summerhill: A Radical Approach to Education*. London: Victor Gollancz Ltd.

OECD. 2004. *What Makes School Systems Perform? Seeing School Systems Through the Prism of PISA*. Paris: Organisation for Economic Co-operation and Development.

OECD. 2011. *PISA in Focus No 9: School Autonomy and Accountability: Are They Related to Student Performance?* Paris: Organisation for Economic Co-operation and Development.

OECD. 2013. *PISA 2012 Results: Excellence Through Equity: Giving Every Student the Chance to Succeed (Volume II)*. PISA: OECD Publishing.

Peal, R. 2014. *Progressively Worse: The Burden of Bad Ideas in British Schools*. London: Civitas.

*Pride School Atlanta*. 2017. "Mission Statement." Accessed 27/04/17. Available at: www.prideschoolatlanta.org/about-us/.

Reay, D. 2012. "What Would a Socially Just Education System Look Like? Saving the Minnows from the Pike." *Journal of Education Policy* 27 (5):587–99.

Rogers, C. 1969. *Freedom to Learn*. Ohio: Charles E. Merrill Publishing Company.

Rogers, C. 1980. *A Way of Being*. Boston: Houghton Mifflin Company.

Rogers, C., and H.J. Freiberg. 1994. *Freedom to Learn*. New Jersey: Prentice Hall Inc.

Säfström, C.A., and G. Biesta. 2011. "A Manifesto for Education." *Policy Futures in Education* 9 (5):540–7.

Santry, C. 20 October 2016. "Children 'more susceptible' to radicalisation under prevent anti-terror plan." Available at: www.tes.com/news/school-news/breaking-news/children-more-susceptible-radicalisation-under-prevent-anti-terror.

Skogen, R. 2010. "The Missing Element to Achieving a Citizenship-as-Practice: Balancing Freedom and Responsibility in Schools Today." *Interchange* 41 (1):17–43.

*Sudbury Valley School*. 2017. "Home Page." Accessed 30/11/17. Available at: www.sudburyvalley.org/01_abou_01.html.

*Summerhill School*. 2017. "Home Page." Accessed 30/11/17. Available at: www.summerhillschool.co.uk/.

United Nations. 1948. *Universal Declaration of Human Rights*. Toronto: Aegitas.

Van Parijs, P. 1995/2007. "Real Freedom for All (1995)." In *Freedom: A Philosophical Anthology*, edited by I. Carter, M.H. Kramer and H. Steiner. Oxford: Blackwell Publishing.

Williams, R. 9 June 2015. "School heads raise alarm over new duty to protect students from extremism." In *The Guardian*. Available at: www.theguardian.com/education/2015/jun/09/schools-duty-police-extremism-anti-terrorism-laws.

Wright, N. 1989. *Free School: The White Lion Experience*. Leicestershire: Libertarian Education.

# 2 Free schools

## A misnomer?

## Introduction

> There are three senses in which schools have been called 'free' schools: free in the sense that they do not charge fees; free from the constraints laid down by the church, state or other authority; and free in the sense of adopting a philosophy of maximum individual freedom for the children.
>
> (Wright 1989a, p. 93)

In 2010, through the Academies Act, a new type of school – a 'Free School' – was introduced to the educational landscape in England and Wales. As of January 2018, nearly 500 new Free Schools have opened, with over 300 more in the pipeline, including mainstream ones, special schools and alternative provision (Department for Education 2018). Described as 'the most overtly market-oriented policy within the Conservative-led Coalition government's school reform programme' (Hatcher 2011, p. 485), these Free Schools sparked huge media interest and a great deal of controversy. In fact, the use of the term 'Free School' was not new. In choosing this term, Michael Gove, then Education Secretary, made explicit links with the 'fristående skolor' of Sweden, but he also made implicit connections with the radical free schools that had existed in England in the 1960s and 1970s. This, according to Gerrard (2014, p. 878), implied a lineage with the 'strong anarchist and libertarian history' associated with these earlier schools. The aims, nature and philosophies of the older and the newer 'free schools', nonetheless, contrast considerably with one another. In particular, they differ in the ways that they might be characterised as 'free', with the earlier versions being free in all three of the areas indicated in Wright's quote (above), and the newer ones aligning with, at most, the first two of these.

This chapter starts by exploring these 'original free schools' and then uses these as a lens through which to assess the 'free' nature of the newer

ones. It argues that the use of 'Free Schools' for the newer ones is a misnomer or a 'red herring' (Leihy et al. 2017, p. 377). It also argues that two
central differences between them relate to whether they offer *freedom to
students*, and in addition, whether their structure, pedagogy or curriculum
can make any claims towards *advancing social justice*. It concludes by pos-
iting that it is more useful to compare the original free schools of the 1960s
and 1970s with contemporary examples of democratic and/or alternative
schools, rather than with the newer incarnations of Free Schools in the UK.

## What were the 'original free schools' of the
## 1960s and 1970s? and how were they free?

In the 1960s and 1970s, amid concerns about the failure of the tripartite
system and an increasing awareness of social segregation brought about
by the existence of grammar schools, a small number of innovative new
schools opened in England and Scotland. These schools, described in this
book as 'original free schools', served working-class communities and were
universally perceived as progressive. They were community-based 'schools
without walls', unrestricted by rigid curricula, school hours or term dates.
Described as 'one of the most radical educational experiments in modern Britain' (de Castella 21 October 2014), they were mostly independent
schools, and almost all of them operated without formal recognition or state
funding. They should nonetheless be seen as credible and legitimate schools
in their own right. Some of these, such as London Free School (est. 1966),
Scotland Road Free School in Liverpool (est. 1971) and White Lion Free
School in London (est. 1972) attracted a great deal of media interest at the
time, and have continued to be a focus of attention for teachers, parents and
academics. This movement in the UK was aligned with a similar trend in the
US, where approximately 800 free schools opened,

> [representing] a remarkable outburst of radical educational dissent.
> Between the mid 1960s and early 1970s thousands of young educators,
> parents, and students themselves explicitly rejected the assumptions,
> aims, and methods of conventional schooling and embarked on experi-
> mental attempts to reclaim authenticity, freedom and wholeness.
>
> (Miller 2002, p. IX)

Of the 14 original free schools that existed in England and Scotland in the
1960s and 1970s, few survived beyond the 1980s. White Lion Free School,
the only one to receive state funding, which was secured through the Inner
London Local Education Authority, was the last to close in 1990. Some
closed as a result of continual problems with funding, or because of other

conflicts and challenges, but it should also be noted that they were also caught up in an educational landscape which was moving rapidly away from child-centred and experimental education and becoming increasingly critical of teachers and local authorities. Margaret Thatcher, as Education Secretary, had already fired a warning shot to free schools, stating that 'It is no good pretending that you can do without standards in education' (cited in Head 1974, p. 11). This was indicative of what was to come, as within a decade or so, with her as Prime Minister, a centralised National Curriculum, competitive League Tables, and a country-wide inspection regime would be introduced. The free schools would have struggled to exist within this changing environment.

Although these 14 schools were all unique in their aims, structures and processes, they shared a number of common characteristics which differentiated them from most other schools at the time. According to Wright:

> They were mostly independent schools, set up on small-scale local initiatives. Most were committed to democratic control involving parents, children and staff. All stressed openness in a number of senses – they were non-selective in their admissions, open to parents at all times, offered their resources to the local community, and tended to open longer hours and more often (including weekends and vacations) than conventional schools. They were open too, in the sense of avoiding closed meetings and not keeping secret files. Few of the free schools made lessons compulsory, and all were committed to non-coercive arrangements. They tended to stress informality and equality between staff, children and parents. In many cases, they cut across orthodox age ranges. And they avoided division of labour, with children as well as staff involved in school-keeping, maintenance, cooking, cleaning, administration, and so on.
>
> (Wright 1989a, p. 96)

These free schools were radically different from other schools. Many drew inspiration from A.S. Neill's Summerhill School (1962), and yet these new schools were based in working-class communities and were free to attend. They were explicitly aimed at local children, and they wanted to build connections with communities. Many opened for longer hours than conventional schools so as to enable parents and other community members to use the school as a learning resource during evenings and weekends. In essence, they were based on the radical philosophies and principles of Summerhill, and yet were not 'fee-paying, residential, rural and [serving] a middle-class clientele' (Wright 1989a, p. 92); they were aimed at working-class children. In addition, these schools did not separate children from communities and families, which Summerhill did as a result of being a boarding school, but rather, they wanted to be *part of* the community.

The story of White Lion Free School is perhaps the most well-known because it survived the longest. It opened in 1972, became funded by the state in 1982 and finally closed in 1990. It was a small school with less than 50 pupils, all of whom were from the local area in Islington, London. According to Wright, it 'hoped to pioneer a radically different kind of schooling for inner-city children' (Wright 1989b, p. IX). His publications about free schools in general, and White Lion in particular, are insightful and offer a unique perspective on the realities of operating within this type of innovative school, widely seen as educational experiments at the time (Wade 10 April 1990). He is not, however, an uncritical voice. In fact, he argues that 'White Lion was an inspired attempt to put radical ideas into practice, but I'm sorry to say that it did not work' (Wright 1989a, p. IX). His description of what happened at White Lion Free School, from his perspective as one of its former teachers, provides a useful lens through which to view 'freedom' and some of the challenges associated with this approach. It is thus important for this book.

Scotland Road Free School, based in Liverpool, opened in 1971, and remained open for four years. It has been described by John Ord, one of its co-founders, as a 'nuclear explosion in educational terms' (BBC Film 1992), by which he meant that it provoked strong reactions from those involved with conventional education, so strong that when the school closed, Ord was discredited and banned from working as a teacher for several years. Scotland Road Free School, along with other schools of this nature, has been described as an 'anti-school' in which 'the immediate aim of the free school was to free those children from an educational establishment that stands for a cynical and exploitative society' (Punch 1977, p. 170). The description of 'anti-school' is perhaps an accurate one when considered in the light of positive and negative freedom.

According to Wright, 'Free schools were much clearer about what they were against than what they were for. Their starting point was a critique of existing schools; the one thing they were certain of was that they weren't going to be like *them*' (Wright 1989a, p. 103, emphasis in original). This aligns with the concept of having *freedom from* external constraint (Berlin 1969/2007), freedom from the notion of what 'school' is and what it should be. This oppositional stance might have been a useful way of attracting interest from those who were critical of current schooling, be they children, parents or teachers, but it proved to be a challenge in practice. At White Lion Free School, defining what the school was – as opposed to what it was not – was a constant source of tension. A commitment to democracy was a central principle, meaning that 'All members of the school community – children, parents and workers – were invited to take an equal part in decision-making. There was no headteacher and no hierarchy within the staff. Running the school was to be the collective responsibility of all' (Wright 1989b, p. 12). Putting these principles into effective working practice was problematic, and there were no pre-established models to emulate. Free schools were pioneers in unchartered waters.

Free schools were sometimes characterised as 'anarchic', with descriptions of children who 'spent hours jumping on to old mattresses, smoking or simply wandering the building' (de Castella 21 October 2014). Even Wright's account, written from the perspective of an insider, alludes to frequent problems with bullying, theft and damage to school property. He attributes some of these issues to the high turnover of staff and children, meaning that the depth of relationships that were needed in order for egalitarian and democratic processes to function effectively did not exist in high enough numbers; there was not a critical mass of children – or workers – who had been inculcated into the culture to make it work in practice. There was freedom, but the concept of *negotiated* or *responsible* freedom (as defined in Chapter One) appears to have been harder to embed. Although students might be seen as having both positive and negative freedom, they appeared to lack the real freedom (agency) (Van Parijs 1995/2007) that was needed to be able to effectively engage with these otherwise hypothetical freedoms.

The freedom that students experienced at White Lion Free School was, in theory, extensive. They were, in many ways, free to do whatever they wanted. Although not absolute, there were very few constraints in place to limit students (apart from those agreed in community meetings). No activities were compulsory. The school did not use coercion of any sort. The students had complete freedom of movement. One former pupil, Jenny, reflects on her experience (Auster 2008). Although largely positive, particularly in relation to 'the collective approach to decision-making' and 'the way that if anyone showed an interest in a particular topic the school would organise trips or a visiting speaker', she also felt that 'that there was too much choice, especially for younger kids who were perhaps not really ready to make decisions around their learning'.

The use of school meetings appears to have been a particular challenge at White Lion Free School. These meetings – based on the infamous Summerhill General Meeting – were sometimes a 'turbulent gathering' which 'could not be relied upon', with issues of authority, power and responsibility frequently discussed but never effectively resolved (Wright 1989b). Maintaining an appropriate balance between freedom and license for the students seems to have been an ongoing concern, with decisions being made but not enacted, or with meetings being dominated by a 'clique'. The details of self-governing processes will be discussed further in Chapter Five.

White Lion Free School did grapple directly with the dilemmas of offering 'freedom from' and 'freedom to'. In one of their own policy documents, they stated that:

> this freedom is not a simple thing. It is not, contrary to the stereotype which the words 'free school' have come to suggest, merely a negative freedom. It is not simply a matter of lifting the constraints of mass schooling, though that is an essential condition . . . freedom must have positive dimensions too. It must be the freedom to make significant choices between positive activities. . . . If such choices, in great variety and closely geared to the children's own experiences of life were not available, 'freedom' we believe would be a meaningless – perhaps destructive – gift.
>
> (White Lion Free School Bulletin 2, p. 6,
> cited in Wright 1989b, p. 27)

This was similar at Scotland Road Free School, where, according to Ord, 'the main problem with freedom is accepting it because accepting freedom, accepting what it really means, is a frightening thing . . . if you really did accept the full message of it, you'd have to change your life' (Ord 1971, cited in BBC Film 1992). He also emphasised that 'the kids also find it hard to accept freedom and what it really means because they sometimes confuse it with license' (Ord 1971, cited in BBC Film 1992).

The question of what freedom meant, and how it could be used effectively, was one that troubled the free schools in the US as well as those in the UK. According to Miller, 'many free school enthusiasts were so determined to reject authority that in many cases they celebrated freedom excessively' (Miller 2002, p. 174). This implies a leaning towards *absolute* freedom rather than *responsible* freedom, a concept that has been critiqued and rejected in the first chapter of this book. In a US context, it has also been argued that 'most people were more concerned with personal freedom than radical social change' (Miller 2002, p. 29). This is perhaps indicative of the social and political context of the US at the time. The free schools that opened there were largely established in middle-class areas, and their cohorts of students reflected this. To some extent, they had more parallels with Summerhill than with the original free schools in England and Scotland. In choosing these schools in the US context, parents were exerting their social and cultural capital and rejecting the dominant model of schooling. In the UK, the original free schools must be see in a different light. As most of these opened in working-class areas, they were deliberately designed to offer a radical alternative for working-class children, many of whom had found themselves excluded and marginalised within conventional schools.

Their claims to advance social justice, by offering a counter-narrative of education, must therefore be taken seriously.

The 14 original free schools in England and Scotland were 'free' in that they did not charge fees; they were independent and thus free from many of the constraints laid down by the state; and they offered extensive freedom to students (Wright 1989a). The free schools in the US were largely fee-paying, and so were free only on the latter two of these criteria. The newer post-2010 Free Schools in England and Wales are quite different from all of these.

## What are the post-2010 free schools?
## and how are they free?

When the Conservative Party formed a coalition with the Liberal Demo-crats after the British General Election in May 2010, the Academies Act was one of the first policies to be taken through parliament. It took less than three months to reach the Statute Book. This is indicative of how important it was to the Conservatives. It has been described as the 'political flagship of the Coalition government' (Wiborg 2015, p. 489). Michael Gove, then Edu-cation Secretary (2010–2014), vigorously drove education policy in terms of design and implementation. In one of his many speeches, he argued that:

> We have one of the most stratified and segregated school systems in the developed world. . . . Schools should be engines of social mobil-ity, places where the democratisation of knowledge helps vanquish the accidents of birth. But in the system we inherited, the gap just widens over time. . . . Far, far too many young people are being robbed of the chance to shape their own destiny. It is a moral failure; a tragic waste of talent; and an affront to social justice. We need nothing short of radical, whole-scale reform.
>
> (Gove 20 June 2011)

This quotation is interesting in tone. In contains several words and phrases which might be of interest to those involved with the original free schools: social mobility; democratisation of knowledge; social justice; radical whole-scale reform. David Cameron, Prime Minister at the time (2010–2016), made several speeches himself, arguing that 'We are backing the parents, charities and committed teachers who are trying to make things better and giving them the freedoms they need to transform our education system' (Cameron 2012). The 'freedoms' that were offered, nonetheless, and the 'radical' nature of these reforms, were quite different from those envisaged by the early free school advocates.

The word 'radical' was used frequently in the policy discourse about Free Schools, but it was most commonly used in the context of radical reform of the *system*, rather than in relation to radical *schools* in themselves. On paper, the only constraints on applications for new schools related to 'those seeking to make a profit, preach hatred or teach creationism as science' (Higham 2014, p. 123), and guidance about curriculum options has included specific reference to Forest Schools, Montessori, Problem-based Learning (PBL), Reggio Emilia and Steiner Wardolf (New Schools Network 2017). Several innovative schools have opened as free schools or academies. Two of these were highlighted in a report from The Sutton Trust (Garry et al. 2018), which evaluated the Free Schools Programme and the ways in which new schools have used their freedom and autonomy. The Judith Kerr Primary School in London offers a distinctive curriculum that provides a bilingual education for all students; this school is named after the author of *Out of Hitler Time* and *The Tiger Who Came to Tea* (Judith Kerr Primary School 2018). The Rural Enterprise Academy in Staffordshire offers students a range of courses based in the land-based, environmental and sustainability sectors. School facilities include a zoo, fish hatchery, a working farm and an equine centre, and students can study for vocational qualifications alongside academic ones (Rural Enterprise Academy 2018). Separately, the XP School in Doncaster has been named as one of the most innovative schools in the world (Sycol Ltd 2018). This school opened in 2014 as an Academy and is strongly influenced by High Tech High and Expeditionary Learning Schools in the US. It delivers its curriculum through cross-subject learning expeditions and has been assessed as Outstanding by Ofsted in all areas (XP School 2018). These innovative schools, nonetheless, appear to be the exception rather than the rule.

In 2014, the Department of Education produced a report which included a comprehensive analysis of a survey sent to all Free Schools in England and Wales (Cirin 2014). This report argued that the majority of schools claimed to use 'innovation' by running an extended school day, setting their own pay and conditions and procuring services from a range of providers, but not in terms of using an innovative curriculum. Those that claimed to be offering an alternative curriculum were doing so by including additional subjects (such as Mandarin) or removing conventional subjects (such as Citizenship). This coheres with academic research which has argued that 'innovation in curriculum and pedagogical practices is very limited' (Wiborg et al. 2018, p. 119), with the vast majority of Free Schools choosing to conform to relatively narrow approaches.

Additionally, there is evidence to indicate that some alternative or 'radical' proposals for schools have been rejected at the application stage, including seven with 'Steiner, Waldorf and/or Democratic traditions' (Higham

2014, p. 134). Existing 'radical' democratic schools, such as Sands School, have proactively rejected the option to apply to become a Free School on the grounds that it would limit their freedom (Hope 2012). Any claims that the introduction of the Academies Act allowed for radical reform in terms of enabling parents to choose from a more radical set of school options must therefore be questioned. This argument is reinforced by the findings from the Sutton Trust, which concluded that, 'Far from heralding a radical new model for schooling in England, free schools represent an evolution of the existing academy programme, and while facilitating pockets of innovation, it has not been transformative' (Garry et al. 2018, p. 13).

The Conservative Party's most persistent argument in relation to Free Schools and Academies (of which Free Schools are technically a sub-section) was that by offering 'freedom' and 'autonomy' to school leaders, they would be freed from the constraints placed on them by local authorities and national governments. As a consequence, they would be able to innovate, in line with market forces, including using the drivers of competition and choice. This is illustrative of negative freedom, of having *freedom from* (Berlin 1969/2007), and has been explained as such:

> The drive for greater innovation starts from the premise that government-controlled schools are constrained by bureaucratic regulations, which are inhibiting change, enforcing uniformity and limiting achievement in education.
>
> (Wiborg et al. 2018, pp. 119–20)

In published speeches about Free Schools, and in the Academies Act (2010) itself, the nature of 'freedom' offered to the new Free Schools concentrates mainly on school leaders and how they might use their autonomy (or positive freedom – 'freedom to') to innovate in terms of staff recruitment, the length of the school day, uniform policies, discipline arrangements and so on. In *The Importance of Teaching* (White Paper), a pivotal document which signalled the changing direction of education policy under the Coalition Government, the curriculum is also mentioned in terms of head teachers being able to 'innovate with the curriculum' (Department for Education 2010, p. 53). Increased freedom for *teachers* is rarely mentioned. Increased freedom for *parents* is confined to decisions about school choice or about setting up new schools. Increased freedom for *students* is non-existent. This is important as it is so markedly different from the notion of 'freedom' that was embedded within the aspirations of the original free schools. In many ways, it is a complete reversal of the values that underpinned the original free schools. Research indicates that rather than offering freedom to students, in the post-2010 Free Schools, precisely the opposite has happened:

students experience greater levels of regulation, narrower curricula and stricter discipline (Hatcher 2010; Boyask 2013).

The new Free Schools are part of a market-driven educational landscape, one in which students and parents are frequently described as 'consumers' or 'customers' with the power to exercise 'choice' within a 'competitive' environment. This gives a different emphasis to the role of children and young people within educational settings. Whereas in the original free schools, there was an emphasis on equality, collaboration and the co-construction of educational experiences, Free Schools now operate in a context in which they are inspected, compared, judged, and if they do not demonstrate effectiveness according to a narrow set of criteria (as assessed by Ofsted), they risk closure. Gove made this extremely clear: 'And if they falter, if things go wrong, if there's any jiggery-pokery, schools will close' (BBC Today Programme 18 June 2010). This means that although, on paper, Free Schools have significant amounts of negative and positive freedom, in practice, many lack the real freedom (agency) to put these ideas into practice. This has been demonstrated through research:

> OFSTED inspections act as a homogenising force as the accountability regime coerces schools to comply with recognised and standardised methods and curriculums. There remains a tension, therefore, between the aims of the broader free school project and the principle of public accountability as currently practised.
>
> (Wiborg et al. 2018, p. 133)

The post-2010 Free Schools are thus in an interesting political position. They are the most visible element of the Conservative Party's flagship education policy, with hopes for 'radical whole-scale reform' resting on their effectiveness. Constraints that have been placed on other schools have been explicitly removed so that they have – on paper at least – substantial amounts of freedom. In line with neoliberalism and a trust in market forces, it is intended that they use this freedom to innovate, to take risks, to experiment, and ultimately, to drive forward significant changes in education.

Through the lens of the quote that opened this chapter (Wright 1989a), these Free Schools are 'free' in that they do not charge fees; in fact, they are not allowed to charge fees nor make a profit. They have been freed (on paper at least) from many of the constraints laid down by the state in terms of regulations regarding curriculum, pedagogy, management approaches and employment practices, though this freedom must be seen as limited in that they are still subject to Ofsted inspections and the threat of closure if they do not conform to 'standards'. They do not – and most would not want to – offer extensive freedom to students. This is not part of the aspirations of most of them or of the Coalition Government itself. Gove (2010) made this clear in a speech in which he argued that 'Under this Government we will ensure that the balance of power in the classroom changes – and teachers are back in charge'. The suggestion that these schools are 'free schools' in terms of their claim to freedom, when compared with the original free schools in the UK and the US, is therefore debatable.

## Do these models of free schools advance social justice?

In the initial rhetoric on the purpose of Free Schools, the Conservative Party frequently made clear links to their role in improving social mobility and reducing social inequalities. The Labour Party's Academies Programme, the forerunner of this policy, had the same aspirations (Adonis 2012). This has continued to be part of the justification for their existence and expansion. Nicky Morgan, Education Secretary (2014–2016), described Free Schools as the 'modern engines of social justice' (Bloom 22 May 2015) when she announced plans to open 500 new ones during the course of the upcoming parliament. It appears that through using their freedom to innovate, these models of schooling have been perceived as having the power to address deep-seated issues with social inequality in the UK.

The original free schools in England and Scotland were established on democratic and egalitarian principles that explicitly attempted to challenge approaches used within conventional education. Education was seen as 'social action' (Wright 1989a, p. 109), and the schools were described as having a long-term aim to 'refurbish the culture of the fragmented working-class community and, in effect, transform society' (Punch 1977, p. 170). Given that both models of free school have made claims about the advancement of social justice, it is worth exploring this concept in more depth.

It is important to note that when the phrases 'social mobility' and 'social inequality' are used by politicians, school leaders and academic researchers, they appear to refer almost exclusively to concerns about *school admissions* and *academic attainment* in relation to children of different *socio-economic backgrounds*. This coheres with a vision of social justice which is about striving for a more even *redistribution* of resources, especially in relation to economic disparity (Fraser 1998). Gove, for example, argued that 'the principle motivating factor is closing the attainment gap' (BBC Today Programme 18 June 2010). He drew on the 'success' of Charter Schools in the US and free schools in Sweden in this regard. Academic research has similarly largely focussed on whether Free Schools in England and Wales have attracted pupils from 'disadvantaged' communities (Higham 2014; Morris 2015), and whether the American and Swedish counterparts have achieved what was promised for poorer students (Björklund et al. 2005; Allen 2010; Carnoy, Jacobsen, and Mishel 2005). Significantly, in the main, this body of research does *not* back up claims that Free Schools are mechanisms for advancing social justice in this way. Rather, it has been argued that 'free schools have contributed, along with other school system reforms, to rising social segregation' (Green, Allen, and Jenkins 2015, p. 910).

Although undertaking research about school admissions and academic attainment is of vital importance, these are narrow interpretations of what should be the focus of 'social justice'. When taken to include the importance of *cultural recognition*, the goals of social justice become broader and include the creation of 'a difference-friendly world, where assimilation to majority or dominant cultural norms is no longer the price of equal respect' (Fraser 1998, p. 1). This is quite different from simply focussing on redistribution of resources, as it is also about the social and cultural status of all groups within society. It explicitly acknowledges 'institutionalized patterns of cultural value that constitute one as comparatively unworthy of respect or esteem' (Fraser 1998, p. 3). This approach to social justice is more closely aligned with the political perspectives of the original free schools. They recognised that the pedagogy, curriculum and worldview that were used within conventional schools were inherently problematic for children from working-class cultures; they were controlled by those in power and reproduced existing inequalities within society (Bernstein 1996). The advocates of the early free schools wanted them to be 'run directly by the children, parents and teachers – where they themselves decide what is relevant . . . where the children tailor *their* education to *their* own needs' (Wright 1989a, p. 105, emphasis in original). This indicates an *implicit* commitment to social justice and the 'democratisation of knowledge' referred to by Gove (20 June 2011). Some schools, nonetheless, went much further. The Freedom Schools in the US had a more *explicit* drive to address social injustice. These originated in 1964 as a summer project to offer a radical culture of resistance, with a curriculum and associated pedagogy which was designed to challenge the dominant assumptions – and prejudices – which were built into the fabric of conventional education (Hale 2011; Jackson and Howard 2014). Although not technically named as free schools, the culturally responsive pedagogies (Ladson-Billings 1995; Tate 1995) that were central to these schools has been described as 'transformative education' (Watson 2014) and are illustrative of Freire's (1970) notions of critical, liberatory pedagogies. They are powerful examples of schools that combine a commitment to redistribution with a commitment to recognition. These will be explored in more depth in Chapter Four of this book.

Free Schools in England and Wales do have, on paper, the freedom to uti-lise markedly different curricula and pedagogies from conventional schools. Although they must still provide a 'broad and balanced curriculum', they are not constrained by the National Curriculum or by the requirement to use qualified teachers (Department for Education 2010). As discussed earlier in this chapter, research indicates, nonetheless, that 'substantive innova-tions in curriculum and teaching methods are relatively rare' (Wiborg et al. 2018, p. 129), with Free Schools largely using their freedoms 'in regards to management practices than in respect of curriculum and pedagogical prac-tices' (Wiborg et al. 2018, p. 119). Despite there being some examples of Free Schools that have been innovative in their approaches to curriculum, even these have not, in the main, used their freedoms to offer culturally responsive pedagogies or to challenge the dominant, prejudicial assump-tions that are inherent in traditional curricula. There is even evidence that a large proportion of Free Schools do not comply with equalities legislation in relation to discrimination (Bolloten 2013). This seriously undermines any claims that they are vehicles for advancing social justice and improving social mobility.

It is important to recognise, nonetheless, that although the original free schools had aspirations to challenge deep-seated inequalities in society and to offer radical alternatives for education, most of them were short-lived experiments which did not manage to put all of their ideals into practice. As Wright (1989a, p. 109) has argued, 'It is not possible to say that free schools successfully pioneered the practice of education as social action. They did not last long enough to demonstrate how this might work, nor to develop their theory'. In addition, there is evidence to suggest that some of the original free schools were resistant to research (Punch 1977), and thus, any stories associated with the advancement of social justice are merely anecdotal. What is clear, nonetheless, is that the *notion* of social justice and the underpinning *ideology* on which these early free schools were premised was substantially different from their newer counterparts. The original free schools have more in common with modern-day democratic, progressive and/or alternative schools than they do with the post-2010 Free Schools, especially those which are informed by culturally responsive and liberatory pedagogies. These will be explored in more depth in Chapter Four.

## Summary

In 2010, Free Schools burst onto the educational landscape in the UK and arguably changed it forever. Despite their contentious nature, they have become accepted by most political parties, and none of the main parties is currently threatening to dismantle them. But what does freedom mean to these schools, and how do they use it?

This chapter has argued that the nature of 'freedom' within these new schools is substantially different from how it was conceptualised in the original free schools of the 1960s and 1970s – schools which offered freedom *to students* as well as being freed from bureaucratic constraints imposed by the state or other authority. These early free schools – such as Scotland Road Free School in Liverpool and White Lion Free School in London – had strong resonances with the free school movement in the US, which resulted in the establishment of approximately 800 such schools, all of which offered a counter-narrative of the purpose and value of education. These anti-authoritarian 'anti-schools' were built on democratic and egalitarian structures in which teachers, parents and students could collaborate and co-create the schools that they wanted. Although all 14 of these radical schools closed in the UK, they have left a lasting legacy and can still be drawn on as examples of how schooling might be different.

This chapter has argued that although the post-2010 Free Schools might be 'free' in name, in practice, their claims to freedom are severely limited. Research suggests that most use a conventional curriculum and pedagogy, and thus limit their 'innovations' to issues of management, staffing and the structure of the school day. The requirement that they conform to competitive standards and are accountable through Ofsted inspections further constrains their real freedom (agency) to offer radically different education (Wiborg et al. 2018). One of their stated purposes – to be vehicles for social mobility – has been challenged by researchers, who have argued precisely the opposite (Green, Allen, and Jenkins 2015; Higham 2014; Walford 2014). It could be argued that these new Free Schools are fighting a losing battle 'to the extent that the free-school idea is . . . one that cannot be realized within the state system . . . a "state free school" may be thought a contradiction in terms' (Truefitt, cited in Head 1974, p. 154). The use of the phrase 'Free School' for these newer models might thus be seen as a red herring (Leihy et al. 2017), or as the title of this chapter suggests, a misnomer.

The original free schools of the 1960s and 1970s have more in common with democratic, progressive and/or radical schools in the UK and beyond. For the purpose of this book, it is far more useful to compare White Lion Free School and Scotland Road Free School, for example, with Sands School (UK), Summerhill School (UK), Hellerup School (Denmark), Sudbury Valley School (US), Pride School Atlanta (US) and the Democratic School of Hadera (Israel). It is also useful to consider all of these schools in the light of the Freedom Schools of Mississippi with a view to undertaking an analysis in terms of the advancement of social justice and the use of critical and liberatory pedagogies. This will form the focus of the following two chapters.

# References

*Academies Act.* 2010. Accessed 26/04/14. Available at: www.legislation.gov.uk/ukpga/2010/32/contents

Adonis, A. 2012. *Education, Education, Education: Reforming England's Schools.* London: Biteback Publishing Ltd.

Allen, R. 2010. "Replicating Swedish Free School Reforms in England." *Research in Public Policy (CMPO Bulletin)* 10:4–7.

Auster, J. 2008. "White Lion Street Free School." *Libertarian Education.* Available at: www.libed.org.uk/index.php/articles/337-white-lion-street-free-school.

BBC Film. 1992. "Lessons in freedom: The Scotland road free school 1992." In *BBC Film.* Available at: www.youtube.com/watch?v=nUEjHvy_Xpl.

BBC Today Programme. 18 June 2010. "Gove: 'Greater degree of autonomy' for schools." In *BBC.* Available at: http://news.bbc.co.uk/today/hi/today/newsid_8747000/8747470.stm.

Berlin, I. 1969/2007. "Two Concepts of Liberty (1969)." In *Freedom: A Philosophical Anthology*, edited by I. Carter, M.H. Kramer and H. Steiner. Oxford: Blackwell Publishing.

Bernstein, B. 1996. *Pedagogy, Symbolic Control, and Identity: Theory, Research, Critique.* London: Taylor and Francis.

Björklund, A., M. Clark, P-A. Edin, P. Fredriksson, and A. Krueger. 2005. *The Market Comes to Education in Sweden: An Evaluation of Sweden's Surprising School Reforms.* New York: Russell Sage Foundation.

Bloom, A. 22 May 2015. "Free schools are 'engines of social justice', Morgan says." In *Times Educational Supplement.*

Bolloten, B. 2013. *Do Free Schools Help to Build a More Equal Society? An Assessment of How Free Schools Are Complying with Statutory Requirements on Equality.* London: Race on the Agenda.

Boyask, R. 2013. "Theorising the Democratic Potential of Privatised Schools Through the Case of Free Schools." *ACCESS: Critical Perspectives on Communication, Cultural & Policy Studies* 31 (1 and 2):11–26.

Cameron, D. 2012. "Speech on Free Schools." Available at: www.education.gov.uk/inthenews/inthenews/a00211691/prime-minister-free-schools.

Carnoy, M., R. Jacobsen, and L. Mishel. 2005. *The Charter School Dust-up: Examining the Evidence on Enrollment and Achievement.* New York: Economic Policy Institute and Teachers College Press.

Cirin, R. 2014. *Are Free Schools Using Innovative Approaches?* London: Department for Education.

de Castella, T. 21 October 2014. "The anarchic experimental schools of the 1970s." In *BBC News Magazine.*

*Department for Education.* 2010. "The Importance of Teaching." Available at: www.gov.uk/government/uploads/system/uploads/attachment_data/file/175429/CM-7980.pdf.

*Department for Education.* 2018. "List of All Free Schools: Open or in Pre-opening Stage (January 2018)." Available at: https://www.gov.uk/government/publications/free-schools-open-schools-and-successful-applications.

Fraser, N. 1998. "Social justice in the age of identity politics: Redistribution, recognition, participation." In *Discussion paper // Wissenschaftszentrum Berlin
für Sozialforschung, Forschungsschwerpunkt Arbeitsmarkt und Beschäftigung,
Abteilung Organisation und Beschäftigung, No. FS I 98–108*.

Freire, P. 1970. *Pedagogy of the Oppressed*. London: Penguin Books.

Garry, J., C. Rush, J. Hillary, C. Cullinane, and R. Montacute. 2018. *Free for All?
Analysing Free Schools in England, 2018*. Slough and London: NFER and Sutton
Trust.

Gerrard, J. 2014. "Counter-narratives of Educational Excellence: Free Schools, Success, and Community-Based Schooling." *British Journal of Sociology of Education* 35 (6):876–94.

Gove, M. 2010. *Speech to the Conservative Party Conference*. Birmingham: Transcript.
Available at: http://conservative-speeches.sayit.mysociety.org/speech/601441.

Gove, M. 20 June 2011. "Speech on free schools." In *Speech at the Policy Exchange*,
London. Available at: www.education.gov.uk/inthenews/speeches/a0077948/
michael-goves-speech-to-the-policy-exchange-on-free-schools.

Green, F., R. Allen, and A. Jenkins. 2015. "Are English Free Schools Socially
Selective? A Quantitative Analysis." *British Educational Research Journal* 41
(6):907–24.

Hale, J.N. 2011. "The Freedom Schools, the Civil Rights Movement, and Refocusing the Goals of American Education." *The Journal of Social Studies Research*
35 (2):259–76.

Hatcher, R. 2010. "New Lessons from England's Schools: New Forms of Privatisation and the Challenge for Local Democracy." *Our Schools/Our Selves* 19 (4):79.

Hatcher, R. 2011. "The Conservative-Liberal Democrat Coalition Government's
'Free Schools' in England." *Educational Review* 63 (4):485–503.

Head, D. 1974. *Free Way to Learning: Educational Alternatives in Action*. Mid-
dlesex: Penguin Education.

Higham, R. 2014. "Free schools in the Big Society: The Motivations, Aims and
Demography of Free School Proposers." *Journal of Education Policy* 29
(1):122–39.

Hope, M.A. 2012. "Localism, Decentralisation and Free Schools – Is There a Green
Light for a Radical Alternative Within England's State Education System?" *International Studies in Educational Administration* 40 (1):89–102.

Jackson, T.O., and T.C. Howard. 2014. "The Continuing Legacy of Freedom Schools
as Sites of Possibility for Equity and Social Justice for Black Students." *The Western Journal of Black Studies* 38 (3):155–62.

*Judith Kerr Primary School*. 2018. "Home Page." Accessed 16/06/18. Available at:
www.jkps-cfbt.org/.

Ladson-Billings, G. 1995. "Toward a Theory of Culturally Relevant Pedagogy."
*American Educational Research Journal* 32 (3):465–91.

Leihy, P., H.A. Martini, P.C. Armijo, and J.S. Fernandez. 2017. "Evolution in Freedom? The Meanings of 'Free School' in Chile." *British Journal of Educational
Studies* 65 (3):369–84.

Miller, R. 2002. *Free Schools, Free People: Education and Democracy After the
1960s*. Albany: State University of New York Press.

Morris, R. 2015. "Free Schools and Disadvantaged Intakes." *British Educational Research Journal* 41 (4):535–52.

Neill, A.S. 1962. *Summerhill: A Radical Approach to Education.* London: Victor Gollancz Ltd.

New Schools Network. 2017. *Mainstream Guidance: Curriculum Summaries, Choosing Your Curriculum.* London: New Schools Network.

Punch, M. 1977. *Progressive Retreat: A Sociological Study of Dartington Hall School 1926–1957 and Some of Its Former Pupils.* Cambridge: Cambridge University Press.

*Rural Enterprise Academy.* 2018. "Home Page." Accessed 16/06/18. Available at: www.ruralenterpriseacademy.com/facilities/.

*Sycol Ltd.* 2018. "The Most Innovative Schools in the World." Available at: www.sycol.com/the-most-innovative-schools-in-the-world/#.

Tate, W. 1995. "Returning to the Root: A Culturally Relevent Approach to Mathematics Pedagogy." *Theory into Practice* 34 (3):164–73.

Van Parijs, P. 1995/2007. "Real Freedom for All (1995)." In *Freedom: A Philosophical Anthology*, edited by I. Carter, M.H. Kramer and H. Steiner. Oxford: Blackwell Publishing.

Wade, G. 10 April 1990. "Closing time at White Lion." In *The Guardian.*

Walford, G. 2014. "Academies, Free Schools and Social Justice." *Research Papers in Education* 29 (3):263–7.

Watson, M. 2014. "Freedom Schools Then and Now: A Transformative Approach to Learning." *Journal for Critical Education Policy Studies* 12 (1):170–90.

Wiborg, S. 2015. "Privatizing Education: Free School Policy in Sweden and England." *Comparative Education Review* 59 (3):473–97.

Wiborg, S., F. Green, P. Taylor-Gooby, and R.J. Wilde. 2018. "Free Schools in England: 'Not Unlike other Schools'?" *Journal of Social Policy* 47 (1):119–37.

Wright, N. 1989a. *Assessing Radical Education.* Milton Keynes: Open University Press.

Wright, N. 1989b. *Free School: The White Lion Experience.* Leicestershire: Libertarian Education.

*XP School.* 2018. "Home Page." Accessed 16/06/18. Available at: www.xptrust.org/our-school/.

# 3   Stories of freedom
## Strangers in a strange land

## Introduction

> 'I had crossed the line. I was free; but there was no one to welcome me to the land of freedom. I was a stranger in a strange land'. – Harriet Tubman
> (cited in Bradford 1869, p. 20)

When the original free schools were set up in the UK in the 1960s and 1970s, it was widely acknowledged that they wanted to be different from the more traditional schools that were available at the time: schools which used corporal punishment and strict discipline; schools which divided students on the basis of 'ability', as assessed through the 11+ examination; schools which had clear ideas about how children should behave and how they should be treated; schools in which Heads and individuals teachers were in charge of the curriculum, pedagogy and format of the school day. The original free schools were clear about what they were *not* – they were not 'like them' (Wright 1989a, p. 103). These 'anti-schools' in England and Scotland mirrored an international trend to establish radical free schools in the US and elsewhere, schools which were 'free from state control and the values of corporate capitalism' (Miller 2002, pp. 2–3). Even today, some radical free schools are still easier to define in terms of how they *differ* from the conventional system, such as Sands School in Devon, which has been described by students as: 'unlike other schools', where they had experienced a 'big battle' characterised by a 'teachers-versus-students mind-set' (Hope 2010). By way of contrast, at Sands School, there is no homework; there are no uniforms; there are no compulsory lessons; there is no pressure to conform; there are no detentions or unreasonable punishments. By setting Sands School as different – as better – students are drawing attention to the contrast with conventional schools.

Describing free schools in terms of how they differ from more conventional schools illustrates Berlin's negative freedom – *freedom from* (Berlin

1969/2007). Democratic, progressive and/or radical schools, described here collectively as 'radical free schools', have deliberately set themselves to be free from many standard expectations about curriculum, pedagogy, behaviour, timetables, assessment and rules. They have rejected dominant discourses that dictate educational policies and practices. They strive to be unorthodox. The question remains, though, of what this provides them the *freedom to* do differently (positive freedom)? If usual expectations are removed, then what do these schools do with the spaces that they have created? At White Lion Free School, the critique has been offered that this space created a vacuum where a 'Lord of the Flies' scenario could develop, a space in which chaos ensued and there were problems with bullying, theft and damage to school property (Wright 1989b). In this case, the students in 'the land of freedom' appeared to need something additional to help them to navigate their way through this new world.

This chapter shares stories of how students experience being in two 'radical free schools' that exist today, one in the UK and one in Denmark. These stories have been developed through the re-analysis of data that were gathered during in-depth qualitative case studies (Hope 2010; Hope and Montgomery 2016; Hope 2017). These stories are interweaved with information from published accounts of three other radical free schools and with comments from those directly involved with other radical free schools across the world. The five main schools describe themselves in different ways. Sands School uses the phrases 'democratic', 'innovative' and 'alternative' (Sands School 2018). Hellerup School has been described as an 'open-space school' (West Larsen 2014). The Democratic School of Hadera considered using 'experimental, open, free, innovative, humanist' before settling on the word 'democratic' (Hecht 2011, p. 41). Sudbury Valley calls itself a 'cutting edge school for independent children' (Sudbury Valley School 2017). Summerhill School uses 'democratic', 'progressive' and 'free' (Summerhill School 2017). For the purpose of this book, they are all categorised as 'radical free schools', as this positions them in contrast to their conventional and traditional counterparts.

The stories are presented as a way of bringing life to this book, to show how freedom has been claimed and reclaimed in a number of different schools, all set in different social and political environments. They are not presented in an uncritical manner. They are not unproblematic. They are not blueprints for other to emulate. They are, nonetheless, interesting cases which illustrate the theories used throughout this book.

## Sands School: strangers in a strange land

Clare is 15. She describes herself as having been 'kicked out' of three primary schools and one secondary school. She is bright, articulate and engaging, but she has an issue with being told what to do. She doesn't like 'petty rules' and she doesn't like authority. In previous schools, she was always getting into trouble for 'silly things', for breaking rules that she didn't think mattered anyway, for having conflicts with other students, for being argumentative with teachers. It was her General Certificate of Secondary Education (GCSE) year, and she was on the verge of being excluded from school again. Her family were concerned. It was an important year. She was worried, too. She described herself as 'going off the rails'. The search for a new school began.

Clare's mother heard about Sands School in Devon and thought it was worth visiting, even though the family lived a couple of hundred miles away. Clare recalls her first impression as, 'I thought this was a very strange school when I first heard about it'. Hecht (2011, p. 146) describes how this is not uncommon; students frequently experience the Democratic School of Hadera as 'a new experiential, stormy, and at first glance, disordered world'. Clare uses the word 'hippies' when talking about Sands School. By way of contrast, she describes herself as a 'chav', as someone who follows the latest fashion and is preoccupied with what other people think about her. She says that she likes to fit in with the crowd. Her experiences of being in previous schools, she reflects, had been purely about 'survival'.

Clare initially came to Sands School in Devon on a 'trial week'. This is the standard process for all potential students who want to join the school. In effect, they attend the school for a week, they meet other students, they go to some lessons (or maybe not), they attend the school meeting (or maybe not), they absorb themselves into the culture of the school. At the end of the week, they decide whether they want to join the school on a full-time basis, whilst their case is taken to the weekly school meeting, which consists of all staff and all students (or those who choose to attend) and a discussion ensues, resulting in a decision as to whether this potential applicant can join the school. Clare was not sure whether she wanted to go to Sands School, but she also knew that there weren't many other options available to her. She said she wanted to go. The school meeting accepted her application.

Clare describes stepping into Sands School as being like a 'parallel universe' (akin to being a 'stranger in a strange land'). She explains that 'it was so weird to see students and teachers on the same level, whereas teachers were always *above* the students and they were always *right* in state schools'. The lack of hierarchy and the absence of authority figures feature heavily in her account of being at Sands School. She also talks at great length about freedom, and in particular, how she feels that she can make decisions for herself. This is beautifully verbalised with the phrase: 'Oh my god, I rule my own life at the moment'. This feeling of being free – and of being trusted – is powerful, and she has stopped pushing against authority because she realises that no-one is telling her what to do. When she feels free, she can engage constructively with herself, with others, with learning, and even with the idea of doing exams. It makes a huge difference in terms of her confidence levels, her attitude to school and her ability to form meaningful connections with others.

The way that 'freedom' is described within Sands School is interesting, and at times, can sound contradictory. Students, including Clare, frequently talk about having 'no rules' and yet they also describe their experiences of being in school meetings and having to deal with cases of when students or staff have broken 'the rules'. The freedom that students experience – and they clearly do feel free – is clearly not limitless. Izzy, another 15-year-old student, explains that: 'I think the main rule of Sands . . . I can't remember exactly how it's phrased, but it's pretty much that you're not allowed to make anyone else not want to be here'. Eve, a 14-year-old who spends almost every day in the art room, agrees: 'sometimes it's OK to break the rule if you know it's not going to hurt anybody else, or you know that it's being discreet and it's not affecting anybody else'. This illustrates the concept of *responsible freedom* whereby students have to take account of the impact of their actions upon others (Rogers 1980). Freedom is not absolute at Sands School, nor at other radical free schools. As Gabby from the US explains: 'you're responsible to be true to your own self . . . but not in a vacuum . . . your freedom cannot impinge upon the freedom of those around you' (IDEC Group Interview 2016).

Eve, in spending all day in the art room, is using her freedom to do what she wants – and she is not hurting anyone else. There are no rules which suggest that she should be doing something other than this. She is free to choose how to use her time. In this case, she is not attending structured lessons, but she is definitely still learning. This notion of 'learning' is similar at Sudbury Valley School, where 'the time spent on any activity evolves from within each participant. It's always the amount of time the person wants and needs. It's always the right amount of time' (Greenberg 1987, p. 87). At Sudbury Valley, structured lessons are not offered at all. For them, the decision to ask teachers to provide activities or 'lessons' is entirely in the students' hands. If they ask, teachers will help. If they do not, then teachers stand back.

This approach invites the opportunity – the risk – for students to 'do nothing', but many democratic educators are adamant that this is a crucial component of offering freedom. Saulius, a parent from Lithuania, thinks that 'a very important part of freedom to learn is *freedom not to learn*. Freedom to do nothing. Freedom to stop at any time for any length of time' (IDEC Group Interview 2016). This aligns with the position of Holt, who made the argument that: 'Deny children – or anyone else – the chance to do "nothing", and we *may* be denying them the chance to do " something" – to find and do any work that is truly important, to themselves or to someone else' (Holt 1972, p. 65, emphasis in original).

When Clare first arrived at Sands School, she did not know whether she could trust what she was being told. Could she really *choose* whether to go to lessons? Was she really *free* to make her own decisions? Would people still like her if she didn't wear the clothes she normally wore, if she just acted 'as herself'? These feelings are quite typical for students (and even staff) who are new to these environments, as explained by Holt (1972, p. 78): 'if we make this offer of freedom, choice, self-direction to students who have spent much time in traditional schools, most of them will not trust us or believe us. Given their experience, they are quite right not to'. Clare responded to this new situation by pushing at the boundaries to try and find out where they were. She left the school premises without asking permission. She didn't go to any lessons. She sat around and drank tea for hours on end, just talking to her friends. She turned up to school without wearing her usual levels of make-up. She describes herself as having 'taken advantage of the freedom a lot'; this has also been described as students becoming 'drunk on freedom' (Hecht 2011, p. 148). After a few weeks, or months, Clare started to realise that the freedom was real. She could make her own decisions. She was responsible for herself. She stated that 'they have boundaries but I wouldn't say that they have major rules'. She went on to explain that

> they discuss what they would like to make as a boundary as to, you know, not going too far and over-stepping the line, like you know, missing a year's worth of lessons and then still expecting to be able to go there and have all the perks of what comes with it if they're doing a practical in science, but I wouldn't really say that they had rules, just you know what's acceptable and what's not acceptable, and you should know that from your own common sense.

She started to trust herself. She started to trust others. She started to love being at the school, to the extent that she declared that 'I'm glued now for life to this school'. She had come to accept the parallel universe as being the one she wanted to live in.

Clare's experiences of testing out the freedom on offer are not unusual. Kathie, aged 15, a quiet girl who had previously spent many years in a Steiner School, explained that, 'it can be quite hard for people who've been in a normal education for quite a long time to fit into it at first'. This was reinforced by Amos, aged 16, who said that new students tend to fall into one of two categories, either 'maturing quite quickly, at least in decision-making, so that they're very independent' or alternatively, 'they essentially just go 'round messing about and sometimes in the worst-case scenario, not actually going to any lessons'. This could last for anything from a few weeks to a few months, but over time, most students – like Clare – would settle into the pattern of Sands and would start engaging more constructively in the life of the school and would start attending lessons. This is reminiscent of Summerhill School, where Neill explained that students would sometimes 'fight shy of lessons'. He wrote that 'this sometimes goes on for months. The recovery time is proportionate to the hatred their last school gave them. . . . The average period of recovery from lesson aversion is three months' (Neill 1962, p. 5).

Sands School has a different philosophy of education from many conventional schools. This independent, fee-paying secondary school describes itself as 'the alternative face of education'. It explicitly defines itself as democratic, though it acknowledges that its claim to be so is compromised by the facts that it is: a) small (it has less than 70 students); b) in a rural location in Devon (a small village); and c) has to survive by charging fees. Despite having a bursary fund and keeping fees as low as possible, Sands School is clearly not an example of Fielding and Moss's (2011) 'radical common school for all'. Nonetheless, for those students who are able to attend, this is a radical school in which students experience negative freedom (freedom from), positive freedom (freedom to) and, importantly, real freedom (agency) which enables them to make real choices and decisions. This is both on a micro level (individual level) and on a macro level (whole-school level) (Morrison 2008). In this, it is similar to the Democratic School of Hadera, which sees itself as operating as

> a sort of microcosm of a democratic state, with two main pillars: 1) the aspect of democratic values: giving respect to every individual, child or adult . . . and; 2) the procedural aspect: operation of democratic mechanisms for the management of the community of the school.
>
> (Hecht 2011, p. 56)

Sands School believes that children and young people can be trusted, that they are constructive, that they can make good choices, that they should be free and that there is no place for 'petty rules'. The school is set up as a democratic self-governing community in which students work alongside teachers to make decisions, to implement decisions and to hold everyone to account for their actions. This is not a one-way process: students hold teachers to account, students hold students to account and teachers hold teachers to account. The belief in the philosophy is genuine and solid, and essential to the smooth running of the school.

By using a different set of values to underpin the school, Sands School is able to offer students a *freedom from* many of the things that students found to be constraining, oppressive or challenging within other schools. They are free from the student-versus-teacher mind-set, unnecessary rules, coercive disciplinary systems, compulsory lessons and homework requirements, uniforms and dress codes, competitive assessment systems, standardised curriculum, age-related expectations, ability grouping, the pressure to conform and an emphasis on academic subjects rather than vocational ones. As a result, they experience a *freedom to* make decisions, make choices, take responsibility, be themselves, be creative, engage meaningfully in learning, belong and feel accepted.

For Clare, experiencing these two types of freedom was transformational. She describes herself as 'still trying to shake off ten years' of being at state school, but she can see some changes and even reports that her mum recently said, 'you're a completely different person'. She explains this by saying that 'my opinion on things have changed a lot', and that she now sees herself as a 'happy bubbly person'. In addition, her attitude toward learning has altered. Whereas in previous schools she was excluded – or at risk of exclusion – she says, 'It would be really great if I left with decent marks, which I will definitely try my hardest for'. For her, feeling this was an important achievement in itself.

## Hellerup School: the land of freedom

Oscar is 14 and Freja is 13. They both live in a suburb of Copenhagen and go to their local school, a non-selective publicly funded school for children aged 6–16. Oscar has been at the school since he was eight and Freja joined last year. Oscar says his parents chose the school because 'they like the concept of the school'. He explains that 'they're very creative and they wanted me to learn to express myself and be creative'. Freja's story is different. She had been in another school but frequently struggled in a classroom setting. When she started getting bullied by some other children, her parents wanted to find her a new school, a different type of school.

Hellerup School is unusual. This is not because of its size, its teachers or its intake. It is not because of its curriculum: it covers all the subjects which would be covered in other Danish public schools (Folkeskoles), especially since the Danish government introduced a more standardised curriculum and a system for national testing in core subjects. It is an unusual school as a result of its *architecture* and its associated pedagogies and practices. It was designed to be an 'open-plan' school, a 'school without walls'.

At first glance, Hellerup School has the appearance of being a working space for artists and creatives, with its light and airy environment, its pale wooden floors and its brightly coloured furniture. It looks a bit like the Google offices in California. The school has three floors. It is extremely spacious, and it has no internal doors and no walls to demarcate classrooms. 'Class areas' are deline- ated by arrangements of furniture such as moveable room dividers, lockers and desks. No class area has a door, and students – and teachers – can wander freely from one area to another. The building is designed in the round, focus- sing on a central atrium with a huge set of stairs – wide enough and big enough for the whole school to sit down. Nicklas, a 15-year-old student, explains that 'it's really never been seen before, this type of school; we don't have it any- where else in Denmark'. For those who describe school as a 'cage' (Piotr from Poland, IDEC Group Interview 2016), the experience of stepping into Hellerup School is incomparable. They cross a line into a 'land of freedom'.

The school building houses approximately 660 students, roughly grouped into classes based on age. Lessons here are compulsory, and there is a time- table. When Oscar and Freja go to their class areas and meet with their teachers, there is a theme for each lesson, and there are tasks to complete. In many ways, this is reminiscent of other schools, and Oscar even alludes to his sense that the teachers are 'in authority'. The formality of this structure is in total contrast to Sudbury Valley School, where 'a class is an arrange- ment between two parties' and might even be seen as 'casual, loose, laid back . . . random, chaotic, undisciplined' (Greenberg 1987, p. 23). Even with the structure at Hellerup School, however, students are still adamant that they 'get a lot of freedom'. They choose which tasks to undertake and how to complete them. If they don't like any of the tasks, they can talk to the teacher and negotiate something different. They can work on their own, in pairs, in small groups. They can go inside or outside. They can sit at a table, on the table or under the table. They can lie on the floor. They can hide in a corner. They can set up a den and take all their work in there. They can be still or they can walk around. They can move to another floor and sit with friends who are in a different class. They are trusted. They have freedom to choose for themselves. Oscar usually likes to sit at a table with his friend Aksel, but sometimes he goes outside on his own and lies on the ground. He says that this helps him to think. Freja has tried everything. When she first started at the school, she moved around a lot. Now, she most frequently finds herself in the library on the ground floor, where she can sprawl out on a huge beanbag with her notepad on her lap.

Freja explains that 'it's really really open . . . you have more opportunities to go out and work where you'd rather want to than just sit in a classroom at a table and just sit there for the whole day. You have more opportunities, you can walk around, you can go downstairs if you want to in the library or you can sit on this floor, whatever'. In her previous school, Freja had strug- gled to manage in a classroom setting as she found it difficult to sit still and concentrate on the same task for a long period at time. At Hellerup, she is able to move around and respond more easily to her body's instincts. She is happier. She is focussing on her work. She is having more fun. She is making more friends. She is getting on well with her teachers. Sometimes, she gets distracted and forgets what she is supposed to be doing. Sometimes, the teachers have to remind her that it is time to come back to the class area to talk about her work. Over time, though, she is learning how she likes to work and what she needs to do to make the best of her time.

Oscar and Freja both enjoy being at Hellerup School, but they also both describe how they have to take more responsibility for themselves. They are responsible for making decisions; they are trusted to know themselves and to be able to get on with tasks without direct supervision from teachers. This is not always easy for them – or for others. In fact, Oscar tells the story of one of his friends who eventually left the school because he found it too difficult to be self-directed. He said, 'I can't handle all this freedom; I'm not ready to take the responsibility for my own learning'. Mathilda shares a similar story of someone who wanted more structure, more direction and 'a tighter schedule and tighter rules'. Freedom, it seems, is not straightforward. Hecht (2011, p. 146) describes this as 'freedom shock' and as a 'frightening difficulty'. He explains how students at the Democratic School of Hadera frequently experience this, where they initially feel 'dizzy, flooded with the many possibilities that school offers' but quickly become overwhelmed, which 'causes the collapse of all the child has known previously' (Hecht 2011, p. 146). These experiences reflect the arguments made by Macmurray (1949, p. 19, emphasis in original), where he stated:

> We flatter ourselves too much when we imagine that we love freedom and strive wholeheartedly towards freedom. On the contrary; there are few things that we fear so much. No doubt we find the *idea* of freedom most attractive; but the reality is another matter. For to act freely is to take a decision and accept the consequences.

Students at Hellerup School frequently talk about a period of adjustment, of taking time to get used to being in this new school. Oscar found this easier because he had never been in another school and so had no comparison. Freja took longer as she had to get used to the fact that 'there's not a teacher breathing down your neck every other second'. She also had to discover how she liked to engage in learning. She had never really thought about this before. This is not uncommon, as explained by Gabby, who works with schools in the US:

> One of the biggest challenges, especially in working with kids who are older and have come through a conventional system is when they're

offered freedom they don't know what to do with it because no one's ever asked them before, 'How do you learn, what do you want to learn, how do you want to express that learning?' and there's a great fear of mistakes, they haven't been taught that that's how you learn, . . . so there's that real challenge of, 'We've given you all this freedom' they're like, 'Okay, what? Tell me what to do with this'.

(IDEC Group Interview 2016)

Teachers at Hellerup School try and help students learn to navigate this 'land of freedom' by slowly extending the amount of responsibility that they are expected to take. When they are in the younger classes, the time they get to complete tasks is shorter, and the support they are given to think about how and where they want to work is greater. Katrine, a 15-year-old who has been at the school since she was 6, remembers doing questionnaires at the start of the year with questions like ' "When you do maths what do you do when you solve a maths problem? . . . Do you see it in your head or do you say it out loud?" or stuff like that and that gives you a perspective on how you learn best'. She explains that 'you work a lot more in your class when you're younger, but when you get older you get more freedom to go out and work yourself or work in a group'. Pernille, also aged 15, agrees that 'it's something you need to grow into'.

In order to 'grow into' using freedom, and take responsibility for themselves, students need to overcome the fear of making mistakes, of making the 'wrong decisions'. The importance of this was emphasised by Mahatma Gandhi, who argued that, 'freedom is not worth having if it does not include the freedom to make mistakes'. Offering environments which welcome mistakes (if that is how they are seen) is an essential component of all radical free schools. Saulius, who has a young child in a democratic school in Lithuania, explains that, 'it's important to allow children to even do something that would be later by them considered as a mistake . . . that's how they learn'. Eric, a teacher from Germany, agreed, although he also acknowledged that this could be hard for him. He said that 'a big challenge for me is to hold back with good advice and to let the students try things, make their own mistakes' (IDEC Group Interview 2016). Rogers (1980, p. 305) argued that students 'need understanding companionship from the facilitator [teacher] as they all search for new ways. They need a supporting atmosphere so that they can fail and still accept themselves'. This necessitates that teachers find ways to 'welcome' students into this new land of freedom.

For Oscar, the freedom that he experiences in Hellerup School goes beyond being supported to make mistakes, choosing the way he wants to complete tasks and learning how to use the physical space in a responsible way. He says that 'it's really free and open-minded, and it gives the pupils a chance to explore their creativity and their own specific talents'. He rec-ognises that the *architecture* of the building actually influences the *mind-set* and attitudes of the students. Mathilda, a quiet 15-year-old with a passion for science, agrees with him, explaining that in a conventional classroom, 'you feel like you're almost like trapped in a box'. Her friend Mia, aged 14, goes further, linking this specifically with the architecture at Hellerup: 'it's a free school and it's also very open, it really gives . . . like *symbolises freedom* in some kind of way because it's not closed halls, small halls'. This sense of space – of freedom – is really important to students. The fact that the school has no internal walls and classrooms literally gives them space: space to think, space to move, space to create, space to be. When viewed in this light, 'space' might be seen as synonymous with 'freedom' (Henrik, Sweden, IDEC Group Interview 2016).

Hellerup School has a reputation, both nationally and internationally, for its innovative architecture. Although this level of recognition is undeniably warranted, there is a danger that it masks what is of greater interest – and that is about what actually happens within the school. This coheres with arguments from geographers about the significance of space. Kraftl and Adey (2008, p. 213, emphasis added) argue that 'for architects and their buildings to be taken seriously, buildings must be imbued with the *power to make a difference* to their inhabitants'. The difference that the architecture at Hellerup School makes is that it enables the teachers to use a more engag-ing pedagogy, one that is based on meeting the needs of 'the individual child', of recognising that all students are different and that they need to be treated differently in order to be able to learn and engage. Hellerup School does not describe itself as a democratic school, and it is not when com-pared with schools such as Sands, Summerhill, Sudbury, or the Democratic School of Hadera. On a micro level, however, the pedagogy at Hellerup is imbued with democratic values as it trusts and enables individual choices to make many choices about their own learning. The architecture of the school cannot be understood without taking account of these pedagogical decisions that informed the school design.

Hecht describes an encounter with some architecture students who were visiting the Democratic School of Hadera. One said:

> We have been walking around here for over an hour, and we still have no idea where the principal's office or the teachers' room is. In ordinary schools, it is very easy to recognize those buildings, because they are usually different and prominent compared to the other school buildings.
> (Hecht 2011, p. 49)

Hecht uses the phrase 'evolutionary architecture' to explain the relationship among beliefs, ideals and physical space. The visitors could not find the head teacher's office and staff room because they did not exist. They were not needed. The school was based on relationships of equality and, as such, separate spaces (especially hierarchical spaces) were antithetical to the values of the school. Similarly, at Hellerup School, the architecture was a physical manifestation of the underpinning philosophy of the school.

The architecture at Hellerup School creates an 'open-space school' – a land of freedom – where children and teachers can freely move around, without restriction, which means they can mix with *each other*. This is deliberate. Although class groups are organised in terms of age, there are many opportunities for students of mixed ages to meet together and work together. Oscar describes the school as being 'like one room'. This is also the case at the Democratic School of Hadera, Summerhill School, Sudbury Valley School and Sands School. Greenberg (1987, p. 71) even argues that 'age mixing is Sudbury Valley's secret weapon' and goes on to explain: 'The school has often been compared to a village, where everyone mixes, everyone learns and teaches and models and helps and scolds – and shares in life' (Greenberg 1987, p. 74). Kativa from India describes her experiences of being involved with radical free schools in a similar fashion:

> What we are looking at is a learning community, so anyone who steps into that community is a learner, so whether it is the person who takes care of the gardens or whether it's a parent, or whether it's a teacher or a student or someone who's managing the accounts, everyone has that freedom to learn and therefore has to be part of that learning community.
>
> (IDEC Group Interview 2016)

The usual constraints which separate children from adults, and children from each other, are removed within these environments.

By using innovative architecture to facilitate engaging and interactive pedagogies, Hellerup School offers students a *freedom from* the rigidity that they experienced in previous schools. Students are not confined to one classroom, or to one teacher, or to students of the same age. They are not restricted by teacher-led instructions about how they should engage in learning and how they should complete set tasks. As a consequence, they describe having a *freedom to* make decisions, take responsibility for themselves, be creative, open their minds, make mistakes and be themselves. The level of freedom that they experience is negotiated, and develops as children grow older, but can nonetheless be seen as *real* freedom.

Oscar and Freja are both starting to think about what they will do when they have to leave Hellerup School. Oscar has recently become interested in maths and business and is thinking about going to 'a special gymnasium[1] that specialises in trading and international economics'. To succeed in this field, he needs good academic grades, but he also needs strong social skills. In relation to this, he is convinced that Hellerup School has helped him, as he says: 'this school makes all the things you need to learn further in your life very easy'. He explains that he has had to learn how to communicate with others, and to work effectively in groups, and that this has happened from a young age. For Freja, the future is less clear. She wants to continue to make new friends and to be happy. So far, she is enjoying being in this land of freedom.

## Summary

Holt (1972, p. 85) argues that 'it doesn't make much sense to talk of "giving freedom" to people. The most we can do is to put within reach certain choices, and remove certain coercions and constraints'. This is what the schools in this chapter attempt to do. They are democratic, progressive and/or radical schools which are committed – in one way or another – to providing environments which are imbued with opportunities for students to have real freedom. Two of these, Hellerup School in Denmark and the Democratic School of Hadera, are publicly funded. The other three, Sands School and Summerhill School in the UK, and Sudbury Valley School in the US, are independent fee-paying schools. The stories of these schools have been enhanced by reflections and thoughts from teachers, parents and students in radical schools in countries as diverse as Australia, Brazil, Canada, France, Germany, India, Hong Kong, Lithuania, Poland and Taiwan (IDEC Group Interview 2016). When viewed in combination, these stories offer illustrative examples of what 'freedom' looks like in practice and how it is experienced by students.

When children are freed from external constraints, a space opens up. In this space children and young people can take risks, make mistakes, engage in holistic learning, become themselves, be accepted, belong, create, play, have fun, build connections, build communities, relate to adults as equals, learn about who they are, unlearn about who they thought they were, consider the endless possibilities and potentials that they have in themselves, try out new things and just be. If they do not have the pressure to achieve according to someone else's measures, if they do not feel that they are constantly competing with one another, if they do not feel that they are being pushed down a particular path which is apparently suited to their academic and/or other abilities, then they experience a genuine sense of freedom, of acceptance, of being valued for who they are. They can take responsibility and develop self-discipline and become constructive members of communities. The power of this cannot be overstated.

The schools outlined in this chapter illustrate how the theories of positive, negative and real freedom are implemented in practice (Berlin 1969/2007; Van Parijs 1995/2007). They all reinforce that responsible freedom is a more useful concept than absolute freedom (Rogers 1980). They show how freedom can be seen at both micro (individual) and macro (whole-school) levels (Morrison 2008). They also demonstrate that 'freedom' is a contested concept and that radical free schools hold different values as to what this means and how it should be implemented through policies and practices. There is no single model. There is no blueprint. All of the schools presented here offer a 'land of freedom', but the geography and terrain of these lands vary considerably.

## Note

1 These offer three-year academically orientated upper secondary education in Denmark. They are similar to Sixth Form Colleges in the UK and US preparatory high schools.

## References

Berlin, I. 1969/2007. "Two Concepts of Liberty (1969)." In *Freedom: A Philosophical Anthology*, edited by I. Carter, M.H. Kramer and H. Steiner. Oxford: Blackwell Publishing.

Bradford, S.H. 1869. *Scenes in the Life of Harriet Tubman*. Auburn, NY: W.J. Moses.

Fielding, M., and P. Moss. 2011. *Radical Education and the Common School: A Democratic Alternative*. Oxon: Routledge.

Greenberg, D. 1987. *Free at Last: The Sudbury Valley School*. Massachusetts: Sudbury Valley School Press.

Hecht, Y. 2011. *Democratic Education: A Beginning of a Story*. Alternative Education Resource Organization.

Holt, J. 1972. *Freedom and Beyond*. New York: E.P. Dutton and Company Inc.

Hope, M.A. 2010. "Trust me, I'm a student: An exploration through Grounded Theory of the student experience in two small schools." University of Hull.

Hope, M.A. 2017. "Re-framing 'Attainment': Creating and Developing Spaces for Learning Within Schools." *FORUM: For Promoting 3–19 Comprehensive Education* 59 (3):413–22.

Hope, M.A., and C. Montgomery. 2016. "Creating Spaces for Autonomy: The Architecture of Learning and Thinking in Danish Schools and Universities." In *The Palgrave International Handbook of Alternative Education*, edited by H. Lees and N. Noddings. Basingstoke: Palgrave Macmillan.

Kraftl, P., and P. Adey. 2008. "Architecture/Affect/Inhabitation: Geographies of Being-In Buildings." *Annals of the Association of American Geographers* 98 (1):213–31.

Macmurray, J. 1949. *Conditions of Freedom*. London: Faber and Faber Ltd.

Miller, R. 2002. *Free Schools, Free People: Education and Democracy After the 1960s*. Albany: State University of New York Press.

Morrison, K.A. 2008. "Democratic Classrooms: Promises and Challenges of Student Voice and Choice, Part One." *Educational Horizons* 87 (1):50–60.

Neill, A.S. 1962. *Summerhill: A Radical Approach to Education*. London: Victor Gollancz Ltd.

Rogers, C. 1980. *A Way of Being*. Boston: Houghton Mifflin Company.

*Sands School*. 2018. "Home Page." Accessed 13/02/18. Available at: www.sands-school.co.uk/.

*Sudbury Valley School*. 2017. "Home Page." Accessed 30/11/17. Available at: www.sudburyvalley.org/01_abou_01.html.

*Summerhill School*. 2017. "Home Page." Accessed 30/11/17. Available at: www.summerhillschool.co.uk/.

Van Parijs, P. 1995/2007. "Real Freedom for All (1995)." In *Freedom: A Philosophical Anthology*, edited by I. Carter, M.H. Kramer and H. Steiner. Oxford: Blackwell Publishing.

West Larsen, J. 2014. "Hellerup School: An Open-Space School [Presentation]." Accessed 27/06/17. Available at: www.youtube.com/watch?v=gT-zx0CviUo.

Wright, N. 1989a. *Assessing Radical Education*. Milton Keynes: Open University Press.

Wright, N. 1989b. *Free School: The White Lion Experience*. Leicestershire: Libertarian Education.

# 4 Stories of freedom
## Advancing social justice

## Introduction

> . . . no education is politically neutral . . .
>
> (hooks 1994, p. 37)

This book has, so far, presented the case that schools should offer more freedom to children and young people, and that although this gives them power and with 'great power there is great responsibility' (Churchill, in Parliament 1906, p. dcccxl), they are able to embrace this responsibility. This argument, nonetheless, has an in-built assumption that schools are politically neutral and that they do not need to take account of social issues within the environments in which they are based. This is not the case. Schools are powerful. They play a role in social and cultural reproduction – of transmitting social inequality from one generation to the next (see Bourdieu and Passeron 1977). Advancing social justice means paying attention to both the redistribution of resources and to the importance of recognition (Fraser 1998). Freedom is worth fighting for only if it contains a specific orientation towards equality and social justice. Freedom for its own sake, without considering the social positioning of others and how this might affect their access to the same level of freedom, is potentially dangerous. Having freedom could *exacerbate* social inequality as it could serve as an agent for social reproduction: those who already have freedom end up getting more; those who do not have this end up with less.

It is widely accepted that 'the educational system passes the dominant ideas of society from one generation to the next, in ways that help to legitimate and reinforce inequalities, while at the same time *it is a place where those ideas can be criticized and resisted*' (Baker et al. 2004, p. 59, emphasis added). Advocates of freedom, and those who are involved with radical free schools, have a responsibility to think carefully about how freedom is offered and what this might mean in terms of addressing and/or aggravating social inequalities. These schools have an opportunity to be different from the norm, to challenge dominant ways of thinking and to become beacons of social justice.

The values and principles of radical free schools are based on equality. Everyone is free to participate. Everyone is free to make choices. No-one is disadvantaged because they are older or younger, child or adult. As Neill said, 'my vote carries the same weight as that of a seven-year old' (Neill 1962, p. 45). Equality is deeply embedded within these systems and processes. At Sands School, Hellerup School, and at all the other schools mentioned in the previous chapter, the commitment to equality is explicit. Izzy, a 15-year-old student at Sands Schools, is adamant about explaining this: 'The most important thing is the fact that we're all equal . . . you can't come here without understanding that'. Clare liked the sense that 'everyone's on the same level, so no-one thinks they're better than anyone else'.

It should not be assumed, however, that radical free schools are necessarily socially progressive or that adults in these environments share the same worldview about prevailing dominant power structures and systemic inequality. If teachers in these schools come from a position of 'privilege', they might not even have a political awareness which would attune them to these matters. In fact, with reference to free schools in the US, it has been argued that 'most people were more concerned with personal freedom than radical social change' (Miller 2002, p. 29). This is a pertinent assessment and suggests that the way that freedom is conceptualised and offered within radical free schools could – inadvertently – favour particular individuals or groups of students. If these schools are modelled on modern democracies, then this is perhaps inevitable, as these systems also favour particular individuals and cohorts. All are not equal. This is clearly troubling and suggests that radical free schools need to overtly consider matters connected with inequality and social justice.

Although Nicky Morgan claimed as Education Secretary that post-2010 Free Schools in the UK were 'modern engines of social justice' (Bloom 22 May 2015), research outlined in Chapter Two has contested the legitimacy of this claim. The original free schools of the 1960s and 1970s, nonetheless, were also unable to demonstrate their effectiveness in this regard – despite worthy intentions – as 'they did not last long enough to demonstrate how this might work, nor to develop their theory' (Wright 1989, p. 109). To explore models of radical schooling with a demonstrable impact on social justice, it is necessary to look elsewhere, and for this, an obvious starting place is the Mississippi Freedom Schools. These schools, although not describing themselves as free schools and not being an official part of this movement, nonetheless had many parallels in terms of being anti-authoritarian and in the way that they wanted to equalise teacher-student power relationships. They deliberately set themselves up as different from conventional schools in aims, structure, process and values. They are used here as an example of a form of education which were firmly grounded in freedom but also had a clear social justice agenda, exhibited through a radical curriculum and a critical and emancipatory pedagogy. These schools wanted to use a liberatory pedagogy to build political consciousness, solidarity and social activism.

This chapter starts with an investigation of three models of schooling: The Mississippi Freedom Schools; their more recent incarnations, the Children's Defense Fund (CDF) Freedom Schools; and the UK-based Black Supplementary Schools (BSS). These shed light on notions of *freedom to* and *freedom from*, but also provide clear examples of how curriculum, pedagogies, structures and processes can be explicitly developed to advance a social justice agenda. This is followed by the story of Pride School Atlanta, a controversial and radical new private school which strives to offer LGBTQ[1]-affirming education for all students who want to attend. Although distinctly different from the other three models of freedom-based schooling, there are interesting parallels in terms of how all of these schools critique the dominant (oppressive) model of education and use curriculum, pedagogies, structures and processes to proactively counter this. All of these schools send out a challenge to other radical free schools to consider whether a commitment to 'freedom' is enough.

## Freedom Schools: from 1964 onwards

In 1964, Freedom Schools evolved from the specific social and political context in the US – that of the emerging civil rights movement. They were part of Freedom Summer, a campaign to increase political awareness and increase voter registration amongst black people. The Freedom Schools ran for six weeks and are credited with being a transformational educational experience for black children, young people and adults across Mississippi. It is thought that 41 such schools were run, attracting somewhere between 2,000–2,500 students during the course of the summer (Chilcoat and Ligon 1999). They were staffed largely by white teachers who travelled to Mississippi from the northern states of the US, and it appears to have been as much of a political education for them as it was for the students. They were prime examples of Freire's 'teacher-students with students-teachers' (Freire 1970, p. 61), where power relationships were equalised and all collaborated in the process of education. These white 'teachers' lived in black communities, with black families, and were involved with campaigning for voter registration during evenings and weekends, after their work at the schools was over. Freedom Summer was politically volatile, dangerous and a source of tremendous tension. The Freedom Schools aimed to fill 'a void in African American students' knowledge of their heritage' but also to politicise them and inspire them towards social activism (Sturkey 2010, p. 355). They had a specific agenda to 'prepare them for freedom struggle' (Cobb 2011, p. 110). Many students, families, teachers and activists faced violent assault. Several civil rights activists were murdered (PBS 2018).

The schools were deliberately set up to offer an alternative to conventional schooling. Despite being a decade on from *Brown v. Board of Education*, 347 U.S. 483 (1954), the landmark legislation which ended legalised racial segregation in the US, making clear that the notion of 'separate but equal' was untenable, segregation was still rife across the southern US states, and many black students experienced substandard education in comparison to their white counterparts. This segregation, in itself, had the impact of leading 'black children to believe themselves incapable of learning' (Perlstein 1990, pp. 302–3). The situation in Mississippi has been vividly described by Cobb, one of the founders of the Freedom Schools movement:

> So education – or miseducation – continued to be a basic *political* tool of white power, designed and used to stem black resistance and struggle for freedom rights (and any real progressive political consciousness in whites). In Mississippi and the South that I knew . . . black illiteracy created by deliberate state policy was used as a rationale for denying political rights to the victims of that policy.
>
> (Cobb 2011, p. 108, emphasis in original)

Freedom Schools offered 'freedom from' these oppressive conditions and also 'the freedom to think, to grow, to decide, to be the biggest, wisest man [sic] we can be' (Perlstein 1990, p. 303). These elements of positive and negative freedom are clearly 'two sides of the same coin' (Feinberg 1980); students could not possibly engage in open and free thinking whilst feeling constrained, ridiculed and oppressed by the system. Freedom Schools rejected traditional education 'which often utilized methods like rote memorization and a passive acceptance of the way things were' (Hale 2011, p. 263). They set out to be different, to be political, to be powerful vehicles for student empowerment. They set out to embrace the politics of recognition (Fraser 1998).

Although Freedom Schools were not permanent schools in their own right, they had a structured curriculum and a distinct pedagogy based on student-centred interaction and discussion (Chilcoat and Ligon 2001). These methods had been devised through a conference in New York (see Education and Democracy 2016, for archive material). The schools set out to offer liberating spaces for students, where they could learn about their histories and reflect upon their own opinions, experiences and perspectives. In many ways, their structures and processes mirrored those seen in the original free schools in the UK and US:

> There were to be no authoritarian teachers or didactic teaching methods. Instruction should permit active student participation, encourage students to reveal feelings, provide opportunities for expression, and develop a sense of group responsibility. There should be 'a close student teacher relationship' that would provide 'the chance of dialogue'.
>
> (Chilcoat and Ligon 1999, p. 49)

What is most notable about these schools, for the purpose of this chapter, is their critique of the dominant model of schooling at the time and their proactive approach to countering this model. They used what would now be described as 'critical pedagogy' (Giroux 1989; hooks 1994), as well as a more specific 'culturally responsive pedagogy' (Ladson-Billings 1995a, 1995b; Gay 2002). This 'focused upon black history and black literature', which meant that 'we were introduced to black authors who we didn't know anything about at the time' (Thelma Eubanks, a Freedom School student, cited in Hale 2011, p. 264). They went further than this, also offering students 'an opportunity to study subjects too "controversial" for Mississippi schools in a "free" atmosphere of honest and mature discussion' and to 'develop direct social action projects to improve local communities' (Chilcoat and Ligon 1999, pp. 51–2). In doing so, they were offering a direct counter-narrative which enabled students to engage with their own histories and lived experiences as oppressed communities. This was new. It was radical. It was transformational. It was an example of what Weis and Fine (2001) have described as 'disruptive pedagogies', those in which deep-rooted power relationships and the assumptions associated with these are questioned and resisted.

The Mississippi Freedom Schools operated for one summer (1964), but their legacy has been revived by the Children's Defense Fund (CDF) in the US. Since 1995, CDF have been running a school enhancement programme in many states – northern and southern – aimed at all children and young people, but especially those from black and ethnic minorities. They use college students as mentors (whom they describe as servant-leaders) to run summer programmes. They are not a substitute for school, but a parallel programme which enables children and young people – some of whom have been described as 'unteachable' and 'unreachable' – to fulfil their potential (CDF 2018b).

The resemblances in their stated aspirations with those of the original Freedom Schools are undeniable:

> [We want to help our children develop] an understanding and appreciation for family, for their own rich heritage derived from their African forebears as well as their American experience, the kind of understanding that will simultaneously provide them with roots and wings.
>
> (Dr John Hope Franklin, cited in CDF 2018a)

Although this statement does not make direct reference to political activism or to the 'freedom struggle', there is no doubt that the aims of the CDF Freedom Schools are underpinned by a strong political critique of the conventional schooling system. It has been argued that:

> Similar to the 1964 Freedom Schools, CDF Freedom Schools serve as a counter-narrative for students, parents, communities and the servant-leader interns in contrast to the continued inadequacies of public education for children of color, particularly African American children and poor children. For example, the books in the curriculum particularly provide African American children with positive cultural messages . . . that are largely absent in typical classroom literature.
>
> (Jackson and Howard 2014, p. 158)

In the UK, there is no direct comparison to the Mississippi Freedom Schools or to the CDF Freedom Schools, but there are Black Supplementary Schools (sometimes described as Black Saturday Schools, BSS). These started to be developed in the 1960s, and it is thought that there are over 50 BSS still in operation today. These schools share a similar critique of the inadequacy of the conventional school system to educate black and ethnic minority students about their histories and cultures. The movement 'represents a grass-roots challenge to the racism that Black children have faced in the British school system' (Andrews 2014, p. 57). They 'found their impetus in their frustration with the knowledge assumptions and hierarchies of the existing school system' (Gerrard 2014, p. 887). They continue to be deeply concerned about the evidence on educational attainment and exclusion rates, which suggest that conventional schools routinely fail to meet the needs of black students (Pears 2 February 2013). These schools – like the CDF Freedom Schools – focus heavily on supporting with the development of English and Maths, and they have an explicit aim of enabling children and young people to succeed academically within conventional schools. Even though they operate alongside, and not in competition with, the mainstream school system, it is clear that they – like the original Freedom Schools – offer 'an alternative culture, an alternative agenda' (Chilcoat and Ligon 1999, p. 66).

Pride School Atlanta is not a reinvention of a Mississippi Freedom School. It is not a CDF Freedom School nor a Black Supplementary School. In three obvious ways, it contrasts completely with these: a) its primary cohort is LGBTQ+ students rather than black and ethnic minorities (though these are not mutually exclusive); b) it is a formal school which offers full-time education rather than a part-time school enhancement programme; and c) it is fee-paying and thus is not easily accessible to poorer or financially deprived students. In other ways, though, there are clear parallels. First, it offers a *freedom from* the marginalisation and oppression that students have experienced within conventional schools. Second, it provides a safe space which enables students to have a *freedom to* be themselves, to think, to learn, to argue, to be. Third, it uses a more radical curriculum, pedagogies, structures and processes, which have an explicit intention to address issues of inequality and *advance social justice* (Hope and Hall 2018; Hall and Hope 2018).

## Pride School Atlanta: social justice in action

Megan was born in a suburb of Atlanta, just a 15-minute drive from the birthplace of Martin Luther King, Jr. She has an older brother and an older sister, both of whom adore her. They had been students in the local public schools, and they had done well academically and socially. They had lots of friends. They were both planning to move away from Atlanta to go to college. Jack wanted to train to be a lawyer. Grace was an athlete and wanted to try out for the US team. Megan was very attached to her siblings and to her parents.

When Megan was a very young child, she was happy. She attended her local community-based pre-school, and she made new friends. She enjoyed doing jigsaws, playing games with other children and dressing up. She was a quick learner and loved looking at picture books. Her favourite books were *The Cat in the Hat* (Dr Seuss) and *Where the Wild Things Are* (Maurice Sendak). At the weekends, she visited her grandparents outside of the city, and she played with her cousins. Everyone enjoyed being around her. They described her as lively, funny, sensitive and full of energy.

Megan couldn't wait to go to school (first grade) because she really wanted to learn to read and write. Her best friend, Ethan, was already at school and he really liked it. At the beginning of the new school year, she started at her local public elementary school. This school had a good reputation. It was the same school that both of her siblings had attended. It was here that things began to go downhill for Megan. She started to feel different. Ethan was allowed to wear long trousers (pants), but she had to wear a skirt. He played with all the other boys during break times, but they didn't seem to want her to join in. Her teacher always seemed to expect her to sit next to other girls, even when she didn't like them. She had never really paid much attention to the fact that she was 'a girl', but at school, this seemed to be important. It wasn't important to her. She knew that she wasn't really a girl, not deep down inside.

Megan went through the school system in Atlanta feeling like an outsider. This feeling got worse over time. By the time she was hitting puberty, things became impossible. The pressure to conform was unbearable, and she was becoming more and more aware of how uncomfortable she felt with being labelled as female. Her parents became worried, but they didn't know what to do. They tried to help her to get through by letting her cut her hair short and by reassuring her that they loved her just as she was. It wasn't enough. Her peers at school noticed that she didn't fit in, and she was frequently bullied, especially by the other girls. This included cyber-bullying, which carried on during evenings and weekends, and so she felt that she could never escape from them. She developed mental health problems. She was deeply unhappy. The doctors gave her a diagnosis of being depressed and highly anxious. At the age of 13, she tried to take her own life. The situation felt desperate, for everyone. Jack and Grace had moved away, and they didn't know how they could help anyway. Her parents had no idea where to turn.

Megan's parents refused to send her back to public school because they knew that her needs could not be met there. By this point, Megan was describing herself as a 'feminine male' and had adopted the name 'Dylan' and the 'he' pronoun. They looked around for an alternative option, and by sheer chance, a new school was just opening. Pride School Atlanta was a small, fee-paying school which was due to open in two months. It described itself as an LGBTQ-affirming school in which children, young people and their families would be supported and respected and their identities would be honoured. They were initially cautious about choosing a school like this, especially because it had received some media coverage which accused it of 'segregation' and of 'coddling children' (Owens 2015; Saxena 2015; Novacic 2016). They spoke to one of the volunteers there, who said 'I think it's good to get them out of the environment where they're bullied and beat up. How can anybody object to that?' They signed up.

Pride School Atlanta is an alternative school, a controversial and radical new private school which strives to offer LGBTQ-affirming education for all students who want to attend. It is not restricted to LGBTQ-identified students. They have an entirely open application process. Heterosexual and gender-conforming students can, and do, attend. It is one of three

LGBTQ-affirming schools in the US (the only country in the world to have such schools), but the only one of these which also uses a democratic free school model. This means that its curriculum is run in a way to be able to cater for individual needs. At the point of opening in August 2016, there were only a small number of students at the school, ranging in ages from 8 to 17. Their needs were very different in terms of their academic needs, social needs and personality types. Dylan was one of the older students, having joined the school at the age of 14. He was academically able, and keen to learn, but he also needed to spend time working out 'who he was' and being able to socialise with people who were 'like him'. Pride School Atlanta was able to offer him the 'freedom to' be able to do all of these things, in his own way and at his own pace.

Pride School Atlanta is staffed by a small group of adults, some of whom are qualified teachers and some of whom have other specific skills and experiences to offer. It feels like a community, consisting of many LGBTQ-identified people and other supportive 'allies'. Parents are also actively involved in the school. Relationships between staff and students are strong and relatively informal. Susan, a lesbian teacher, explained that 'we're here to learn and teach at the same time'. This egalitarian, non-hierarchical and informal culture is reminiscent of the Mississippi Freedom Schools, where teachers were frequently described as 'moderators', which meant that 'teachers were to promote thoughtful, personal inquiry and to avoid using their "authority" to influence students' actions' (Chilcoat and Ligon 2001, p. 215). At Pride School Atlanta, students have good relationships with staff, but also – and equally importantly – they have strong relationships with one another. Jordan, aged 12, explained that 'we understand each other better, because we've all been through at least a little bit of the same things, and a lot of us have shared experiences'. Creating this sense of a shared sense of community, both inside and outside of school, is central to the way that Pride School Atlanta operates.

According to the founder of Pride School Atlanta, the decision to choose a free school model was because 'we largely service students who have been under-served'. By this, he meant that 'we knew that every kid would really need to be on their own track, and yes, not base it on age'. This was because many of the students had missed large chunks of schooling and could not, therefore, be expected to necessarily meet age-related expectations. This was certainly the case for Dylan, and for his new friend Madison, who had missed an entire year of formal schooling. Pride School Atlanta also wanted to use a free school model as it would help students to 'find their way back into their education . . . to actually take ownership for it, where it's been taken away from them for so long'. This has resonances with CDF Freedom Schools and with Black Supplementary Schools, both of which attempt to help marginalised children and young people to fulfil their potential outside of and as part of the mainstream school system.

Pride School Atlanta offers a comparable curriculum to other local schools in terms of conforming to Georgia State Standards in core subjects. Although the pedagogy is different in that groups are much smaller and learning is individualised, curriculum content is similar. What differs, however, is their commitment to enabling students to be free to be themselves in terms of self-expression. Madison, aged 15, describes what being at Pride School feels like:

> For me it feels like I'm not chained down and I don't have to hide myself. I can be sometimes really shy and nervous around certain people, but this school kind of just opens that up, like you can come out of your shell here. Like you're not locked in a cell and having to hide who you are. So you're free.

The school wants students to feel confident and to develop pride in themselves. The founder is adamant that this is a central aim of the school because

> that's why most of them are here, because they don't fit, and here's a place where they can develop pride for being who they are. . . . And so, regardless of why you were craving a place where you can thrive, and not just barely survive, this can be a place for you.

The experience of not fitting in was expressed by one student as being about 'self-doubt'; once starting at Pride School Atlanta, they felt 'like a bunch of weight just came off'. In this, there are parallels with the Freedom Schools, which also had a proactive agenda to challenge student's own deficit thinking, much of which has been exacerbated through negative experiences in other schools. In Mississippi, this had been based on deep-rooted systemic racism. In schools today, the assumption of heterosexuality and gender normativity is pervasive and powerful. This, it is argued, is manifested

> most powerfully in the silence that surrounds the subject of sexual orientation . . . the silence denies lesbian, gay and bisexual young people a legitimated social space and language for reflecting upon a defining part of their personal and social identity.
>
> (Baker et al. 2004, p. 155)

Pride School Atlanta provides a legitimated social space and a language. The importance of this cannot be overstated.

Alongside the formal curriculum, Pride School also offer an informal 'queer curriculum' in that teachers are able – and encouraged – to bring LGBTQ perspectives into all aspects of teaching and learning. As one teacher explained:

> Society has made them 'the other', in finger quotes, but there were people like them throughout history, we've just told them to ignore that they existed, because people in the past have been uncomfortable about admitting that people are gay, or people are trans, or that not everyone fits into a nice little box. And if we can give them a sense that who they are is okay, just as they are, and surround them with that message, I think it's almost like sending them out in the world with an Iron Man outfit on, you know?

This clearly affects the nature of formal teaching sessions at Pride School. There is an extensive library of books written by LGBTQ-identified authors or covering relevant themes. Students are able to ask for particular sessions to be offered which focus on issues that particularly interest them. Teachers feel free, too. As one stated: 'I'm excited about the opportunity to teach the whole story instead of the politically correct version of history'. They no longer have to 'whitewash' or 'edit' curriculum content, which is a direct contrast to their experiences in previous schools, where some of them were explicitly instructed to remove any references to gender and sexuality from the curriculum. This sense of teaching the 'whole story' has clear parallels with the way that the original Freedom Schools, the CDF Freedom Schools and the Black Supplementary Schools have also designed their curricula. It is liberating for teachers as well as for students.

Equally, or possibly more significant, is the 'queer curriculum' that takes place on a more informal, conversational, human-to-human level. This was described by the founder of the school as 'the queer studies is happening right in front of them . . . that's *social justice in action*, you know'. All of the adults at Pride School Atlanta are LGBTQ-identified or are supportive allies, and this in itself provides educational opportunities for young people. Michael, a gay male teacher, explained the impact of this: 'they see us walk through the door every other day or every day or whatever, and here we are, we're living, breathing people who engage in their world and say, "Yes, this is who we are. We're openly gay or allied"'. This was important to Dylan, and to the other students, who frequently used the phrase 'people like us' to refer to adults and other students at Pride School Atlanta. The same sense of connection – and of the safety that comes from this – has been identified in relation to Black Supplementary Schools. Andrews (2014, pp. 59–61) argues that 'one of the main successes of Supplementary Schools is the Black-led environment of the programmes. . . . it is impossible to overestimate the strength of the Black-led environment in creating a comfortable space'. These types of environments, quite different from conventional schools, create a sense of community, safety and solidarity (see Hope and Hall 2018).

Dylan was able to be reflective about his experiences of being in other schools. He had felt constrained, scared and anxious. He felt that he was not able to be himself, as the environment was not safe enough to support him in this goal. His mother concurred with this, saying, 'You are kind of safe in class, if the teacher is paying attention. If the teacher has her back turned, maybe not, but for most time, you are kind of safe when you are actually in class, but lunch, before school, walking to the bus after school, lockers, between classes, gym locker room, cafeteria. There is no safety'. She had heard stories about Dylan's experiences of bullying, and she had seen the impact of this on his mental health. They were not dissimilar experiences to other students at Pride School Atlanta, some of whom had feared for their physical safety. Jayden, a confident 14-year-old with a passion for studying art history, stated that, 'I'm not waking up every day scared that I'm going to get here and I'm going to get beat up, or I'm going to get, you know, a knife pulled on me in the bathroom'. The use of bathrooms was a particular concern for several students, an increasingly politicised issue which had, of course, been played out on the national stage during the 2016 US Presidential Campaign. Over time, in his previous schools, Dylan had become increasingly withdrawn and isolated, and as a result, he was not able to engage in academic work. At Pride School Atlanta, his experiences felt completely different. He explained that: 'when there's nobody here that would like physically hurt me or, you know, bully me on purpose. . . . Because like I don't worry about what's going to happen to me here all the time, so instead of my mind being filled with that, *it has space for work*'. He was experiencing a 'freedom to learn'.

By the end of the first year, Dylan felt more comfortable with who he was and who he wanted to be. Rather than constraining him and putting a label on him, Pride School Atlanta had done precisely the opposite. During the course of the year, Dylan had become less attached to his gender identity as being either male or female, and had experimented with using a range of different pronouns – he, she and they. He could only do this, he explained, because he was 'free from' any expectations of what these labels meant. He could wear a leather jacket on one occasion and a cropped top on another. There were no pressures on him, no expectations of how he was expected to behave. He says that 'I appreciate like, the openness of the space that you have, to be able to change yourself in, you know like grow yourself without judgement and stuff'. This could have only happened at Pride School

Atlanta, he explained, as conventional schools (and society in general) wanted to 'put you in a box'. By attending an LGBTQ-affirming school in which all identities were welcomed, he had felt free of expectation.

By using a different set of values to underpin the school, Pride School Atlanta is able to offer students a *freedom from* many of the things that students found to be constraining, oppressive or challenging within other schools. They are free from gender-normative expectations; rules about pronouns, names, uniforms and bathrooms; unsafe environments, especially public spaces; homophobic and heteronormative policies and practices; curriculum which silences them and doesn't tell the 'whole story'. As a result, they experience a *freedom to* be themselves, experiment, learn from each other, label or not label themselves, engage meaningfully in learning, belong and feel accepted.

For Dylan, experiencing these two types of freedom were personally transformational, so much so that he describes the school as being 'a life-saver' (literally). After a year at the school, he decided that he wanted to stay at the school, but he was also considering re-entering the public school system in the future. This, he felt, would offer him greater opportunities to pursue his dream of being a scientist. He felt able to consider doing this now, he explained, because he knew who he was, and he felt confident that he could challenge the school if he started to feel he was being treated unreasonably. He was ready.

## Summary

Education is not politically neutral. Gorard and See (2013, p. 48) contend that 'schools, in their structure and organisation, can represent to young people the kind of society that we wish to have, rather than reflecting the inequalities of the society we actually have'. This places a responsibility on all schools, including radical free schools, to consider the types of society that they wish to have, and to find ways of modelling these types.

The Mississippi Freedom Schools, CDF Freedom Schools, Black Supplementary Schools and Pride School Atlanta are all committed to providing a different kind of schooling for children and young people – schooling which takes account of the dominant discourses in conventional education and attempt to challenge these ideas. These schools strive to counter systemic inequalities on grounds of 'race', gender, sexual orientation, disability and so on. They aim to build self-esteem, self-confidence and strong identities amongst students. They reconceptualise curriculum and pedagogies to account for the 'whole story' of humanity, to fill the gaps that are endemic within conventional schooling. In short, they hold and advance an explicit social justice perspective.

Radical schools do not operate in a vacuum. They are part of particular social and political contexts. Adults, children and young people within these environments are also members of other communities and a wider society. The schools, therefore, have a responsibility to take account of the social and political inequalities which are embedded within the context in which they operate. This is a massive task. On their own, they cannot transform society, but they can play a role in increasing political awareness and understanding – of an engendered sense of the 'freedom struggle'. This entails a major re-thinking of whether offering 'freedom' is enough or whether it needs to be accompanied by a deeper political agenda.

The price of holding an orientation towards freedom is that – in some cases – adults might make decisions which limit the freedom of children and young people. They might decide, for example, that some elements of the curriculum should be compulsory, especially in terms of focussing on developing social, cultural and political understanding. They might decide that particular policies and procedures are non-negotiable, including those relating to admission policies, to offering bursaries or to bullying. They might make decisions about employing pedagogies which are liberating and utilise critical pedagogy and culturally responsive teaching. This price is worth paying. Education is not politically neutral. Radical free schools aspire to be different from conventional schools, and by making proactive decisions which advance social justice, they have an opportunity – a real freedom – to make an impact.

## Note

1  LGBTQ refers to lesbian, gay, bisexual, transgendered and queer. The acronym used by Pride School Atlanta usually also includes QIAA, which is questioning, intersex, asexual and allies. This is sometimes abbreviated to LGBTQ+.

## References

Andrews, K. 2014. "Resisting Racism: The Black Supplementary School Movement." In *Alternative Education and Community Engagement*, edited by O.D. Clennon. Basingstoke: Palgrave MacMillan.

Baker, J., K. Lynch, S. Cantillon, and J. Walsh. 2004. *Equality: From Theory to Action*. Hampshire: Palgrave MacMillan.

Bloom, A. 22 May 2015. "Free schools are 'engines of social justice', Morgan says." In *Times Educational Supplement*.

Bourdieu, P., and J-C. Passeron. 1977. *Reproduction in Education, Society and Culture*. London: Sage.

CDF. 2018a. "Freedom Schools Reborn: The CDF Freedom Schools Program Model." Children's Defense Fund. Accessed 22/02/18. Available at: www.childrens defense.org/programs/freedomschools/.

CDF. 2018b. "Program Impact." Accessed 22/08/18. Available at: www.childrens defense.org/programs/freedomschools/.

Chilcoat, G.W., and J.A. Ligon. 1999. "Helping to Make Democracy a Living Reality: The Citizenship Curriculum of the Mississippi Freedom Schools." *Journal of Curriculum and Supervision* 15 (1):43–68.

Chilcoat, G.W., and J.A. Ligon. 2001. "Discussion as a Means for Transformative Change: Social Studies Lessons from the Mississippi Freedom Schools." *The Social Studies* :213–9.

Cobb, C. 2011. "Freedom's Struggle and Freedom Schools." *Monthly Review* July-August:104–13.

*Education and Democracy.* 2016. "Freedom School Curriculum." Accessed 20/02/18. Available at: http://educationanddemocracy.org/ED_FSC.html.

Feinberg, J. 1980. *Rights, Justice and the Bounds of Liberty.* New Jersey: Princeton University Press.

Fraser, N. 1998. "Social justice in the age of identity politics: Redistribution, recognition, participation." In *Discussion paper // Wissenschaftszentrum Berlin für Sozialforschung, Forschungsschwerpunkt Arbeitsmarkt und Beschäftigung, Abteilung Organisation und Beschäftigung, No. FS I 98–108.*

Freire, P. 1970. *Pedagogy of the Oppressed.* London: Penguin Books.

Gay, G. 2002. "Preparing for Culturally Responsive Teaching." *Journal of Teacher Education* 53 (2):106–16.

Gerrard, J. 2014. "Counter-narratives of Educational Excellence: Free Schools, Success, and Community-Based Schooling." *British Journal of Sociology of Education* 35 (6):876–94.

Giroux, H.A. 1989. *Schooling for Democracy: Critical Pedagogy in the Modern Age.* London: Routledge.

Gorard, S., and B.H. See. 2013. *Overcoming Disadvantage in Education.* Oxon: Routledge.

Hale, J.N. 2011. "The Freedom Schools, the Civil Rights Movement, and Refocusing the Goals of American Education." *The Journal of Social Studies Research* 35 (2):259–76.

Hall, J.J., and M.A. Hope. 2018. "Lost in Translation: Naming Practices and Public Feelings Towards 'Gay Schools'." In *Youth Sexualities: Public Feelings and Contemporary Cultural Politics,* edited by S. Talburt. California: Praeger.

hooks, b. 1994. *Teaching to Trangress: Education as the Practice of Freedom.* Oxon: Routledge.

Hope, M.A., and J.J. Hall. 2018. " 'This Feels like a Whole New Thing': A Case Study of a New LGBTQ-affirming School and Its Role in Developing 'Inclusions'." *International Journal of Inclusive Education.* DOI: 10.1080/13603116.2018.1427152. Available at: www.tandfonline.com/doi/full/10.1080/13603116.2018.1427152.

Jackson, T.O., and T.C. Howard. 2014. "The Continuing Legacy of Freedom Schools as Sites of Possibility for Equity and Social Justice for Black Students." *The Western Journal of Black Studies* 38 (3):155–62.

Ladson-Billings, G. 1995a. "But That's Just Good Teaching! The Case for Culturally Relevent Pedagogy." *Theory into Practice* 34 (3):158–65.

Ladson-Billings, G. 1995b. "Toward a Theory of Culturally Relevant Pedagogy." *American Educational Research Journal* 32 (3):465–91.

Miller, R. 2002. *Free Schools, Free People: Education and Democracy After the 1960s*. Albany: State University of New York Press.

Neill, A.S. 1962. *Summerhill: A Radical Approach to Education*. London: Victor Gollancz Ltd.

Novacic, I. 2016. "New LGBTQ school joins battle for trans rights in America." In *CBS News*. Available at: www.cbsnews.com/news/new-lgbtq-school-joins-battle-for-trans-rights-in-america/.

Owens, E. 2015. "Atlanta Gay School Organizers Hope To Segregate Gay Students into Gay Ghetto." In *The Daily Caller*. Available at: http://dailycaller.com/2015/02/18/atlanta-gay-school-organizers-hope-to-segregate-gay-students-into-gay-ghetto/.

Parliament, Great Britain. 1906. *The Parliamentary Debates*. London: Reuter's Telegram Company.

PBS. 2018. "Murder in Mississippi." In *American Experience Collection*. Available at: www.pbs.org/wgbh/americanexperience/features/freedomsummer-murder/.

Pears, E. 2 February 2013. "Are black children failing in school?" In *The Voice*.

Perlstein, D. 1990. "Teaching Freedom: SNCC and the Creation of the Mississippi Freedom Schools." *History of Education Quarterly* 30 (3):297–324.

Saxena, V. 2015. "Pride School Atlanta: New Private School to Cater Only to 'Queer and Trans Families'." In *Downtrend.com*. Available at: http://downtrend.com/vsaxena/pride-school-atlanta.

Sturkey, W. 2010. " 'I Want to Become a Part of History'; Freedom Summer, Freedom Schools and the Freedom News." *The Journal of African American History* 95 (3–4):348–68.

Weis, L., and M. Fine. 2001. "Extraordinary Conversations in Public Schools." *International Journal of Qualitative Studies in Education* 14 (4):497–523.

Wright, N. 1989. *Assessing Radical Education*. Milton Keynes: Open University Press.

# 5 Freedom and self-governance

## Introduction

> Crucial is the recognition that conditions must be deliberately created to enable the mass of people to act on their power to choose.
>
> (Greene 1988, p. 18)

This book presents the argument that children and young people should have more freedom, and that when given this freedom, they can be trusted to use it. A number of different types of freedom have been identified, including negative freedom (freedom from) and positive freedom (freedom to) (Berlin 1969/2007). Lists could be offered of what might constitute positive freedom, including freedom to speak, freedom to create, freedom to be, freedom to think, freedom to become, freedom to be accepted, freedom to explore, freedom to develop and freedom to learn (for examples of such lists, see Montgomery and Hope 2016; Freedom to Learn Project 2017). It has further been claimed that children and young people need real freedom (agency) to be able to experience these in practice (Van Parijs 1995/2007). They need to be able to feel that they have the opportunity – the power – to be able to enact these otherwise hypothetical freedoms.

This chapter argues that the positive 'freedoms' named earlier – including freedom to think, freedom to create, freedom to be and freedom to learn – are all included under the overarching umbrella of 'freedom to choose'. The matter of making choices, of making *real* choices, of being involved in genuine decision-making, is a cornerstone of freedom. This is so central that it warrants detailed examination.

Radical free schools often stand apart from more conventional schools in that they enable children and young people – sometimes those as young as five – to be seriously and actively involved in decision-making, in *self-governance*. This self-governance is two-fold. First, children and young people are trusted to make choices in relation to themselves and to their engagement in school and in learning. This might be characterised as being about *personal autonomy*, independence and personal agency. This is self-governance if the word 'self' is taken to be a personal and individual characteristic – a micro level of freedom (Morrison 2008). The radical free schools included in this book place great value on enabling children and young people to make micro-level decisions, be that through having freedom to choose where and how to work (Hellerup School), whether to attend lessons (Summerhill School, Sands School, Sudbury Valley School) or which names and pronouns to use (Pride School Atlanta). Second, children and young people can be enabled, through deliberate and explicit structures and processes, to be actively involved in *collective decision-making* about the school as a whole. This is still linked with personal agency, but it is also about others, about democracy, community, connection and belongingness – a macro level of freedom (Morrison 2008). Many of the radical free schools identified in this book, especially those described as 'democratic', are committed to self-governance of this nature and have created mechanisms to enable this to take place. Summerhill School, Sands School, the Democratic School of Hadera, Sudbury Valley School and Pride School Atlanta all have whole-school meetings and a variety of other processes for engaging children and young people in school-level decisions. This second aspect of community or collective decision-making uses the 'self' of self-governance to refer to a community experience, a 'conjoint communicated experience' through 'a mode of associated living' (Dewey 2004, p. 83).

The original Free Schools of the 1960s and 1970s placed great emphasis on the importance of self-governance, and most used the format of weekly school meetings to bring 'the community' together to make decisions. This was a significant innovation in the political context of the time, where in most schools, students were not able to make even the most rudimentary of decisions about their own lives and their own learning, let alone being involved with school-level decisions. Inspired by Neill and Summerhill, White Lion Free School had an explicit commitment to democracy and held two weekly meetings, one for children and one for staff/parents (although children, staff and parents could actually attend either meeting). Decisions were made largely by consensus. The experiences of those at White Lion Free School, however, were not easy. Implementing school meetings was a radical act when compared with its counterparts, but it appears as if it was deeply flawed as a practical project in terms of managing effective self-governance. Wright explains that:

> For some youngsters, these meetings were a valuable learning experience. They learned, for example, how to command the attention of a

turbulent gathering; how to use diplomacy and tact; how to argue a case; how to sort out relevant considerations from irrelevant ones; how to disarm bullies; how to perceive ways out of predicaments and formulate workable solutions. For them the shortcomings of the meetings were not an obstacle to learning, but rather an opportunity for learning how to operate effectively in a difficult environment. But for the majority of children the meetings were frustrating and something to get over with as soon as possible. Under these conditions it cannot be said that 'self government' was being realised in any meaningful sense.

(Wright 1989b, p. 15)

Wright's analysis of the issues at White Lion is that although students were involved in *making* the decisions, the responsibility for *enforcing* them appeared, by default, to fall to the staff members. Students were law-makers but not law-enforcers. Power had been shared on the one hand, but remained firmly with the teachers on the other. Although he acknowledges that 'it was usually possible to arrive at a conclusion which was tolerably acceptable to everyone' (Wright 1989b, p. 16), he also describes the meetings as 'chaotic'. These descriptions are far from a ringing endorsement of using 'democratic' meetings as self-governance mechanisms.

The experiences of the original free schools draw attention to some important questions to consider in relation to enabling children and young people to effectively make use of having a 'freedom to choose' – of being involved in self-governance. First, how might they be supported to make choices on an individual level; second, what mechanisms might be used to enable effective decision-making on a whole-school level (and in particular, are there alternatives to a simple 'one-person-one-vote system'); third, at what age should children and young people be deemed able to be fully involved in decision-making on either an individual or group level? Addressing these questions will form the basis of this chapter.

## How can children and young people be supported to have 'freedom to choose' and develop personal autonomy?

The development of autonomy has been characterised as being a central goal of education because 'no learner can be effective in more than a very limited area if he or she cannot make decisions for themselves about what they should be learning and how they should be learning it' (Boud 1988, p. 17). In this context, autonomy can be taken to mean 'the capacity of human beings to reason self-consciously, to be self-reflective and to be self-determining' (Held 2006, p. 263). It is frequently linked with being an independent learner, with being self-directed, with being able to take responsibility for one's own learning. Many schools – including conventional ones – seek to support students to develop as autonomous *learners*. Radical free schools frequently take this support one step further (or several steps further) and overtly aspire to support students to become autonomous *beings*.

Becoming autonomous necessitates being able to make decisions, personalised individual choices which are not overly influenced by input from others. The word 'autonomy' originates from '*autos* (self) and *nomos* (rule or law)' (Dworkin 2007, p. 333) and has been described as being 'self-legislation, or obeying only one's own rules' (Carter, Kramer, and Steiner 2007, p. 323). To develop such capacities, it is essential that individuals feel able to make choices. For children and young people, especially those who have not been given such freedom before, this can prove challenging.

Offering children and young people a 'freedom to choose' does not necessarily mean that they have entire control over all decisions. This would be *absolute freedom*, which as this book has already argued, is an unhelpful concept. In *Freedom to Learn* (1969, p. 11), Rogers (1980, p. 305) uses the phrase *responsible freedom* to refer to the type of freedom offered within educational institutions. He tells the story of Miss Shiel's experiments with offering freedom to primary school children, explaining that 'she risked giving freedom to her pupils only so far as she dared, only so far as she felt reasonably comfortable in doing so'. The ensuing tale is one in which children were able to make many choices and self-direct their own learning within an unstructured classroom, supported by the use of individually negotiated work contracts and continual self-evaluation. After a week, those children who were struggling to meaningfully engage in learning were moved into a small teacher-directed group for a short while, until they were better able to cope with the responsibilities that came along with their freedom to make choices.

As has already been illustrated (in Chapter Three), students in radical free schools frequently experience 'freedom shock', which means they struggle with the new-found freedom which contrasts so dramatically with their previous experiences of schooling. This has been described as 'going off the rails' (Clare, age 15, Sands School) and as being 'something you need to grow into' (Pernille, age 15, Hellerup School). Although each individual student's experience is entirely unique, there are remarkable similarities in some of the stories, and narratives of how students can get 'drunk on freedom' reverberate across the globe (IDEC Group Interview 2016). For teachers, the experiences of being involved in schools which are committed to freedom can be equally challenging. Holt (1972, p. 9) refers to 'some of the difficulties and tensions we meet when we try to create situations in which learners are free to learn' as 'new, strange, awkward, perplexing, even threatening'.

One way to support children and young people – and teachers – to adjust to these types of environments is to slowly introduce opportunities for students to develop skills and confidence in decision-making. This is explained by Holt:

> When we first try to open up our classrooms it may make the change easier for everyone if instead of offering a wide choice from the start, we widen the range of choices very gradually. If we say to a student used to traditional classes, 'Now you may choose to do anything you want', he may do nothing. If instead we say, 'You can choose between these two or three possibilities', he may be more able to choose. Next time we can offer four or five choices.
>
> (Holt 1972, p. 87)

Teachers and facilitators, therefore, can experiment with offering a degree of freedom to children (as individuals and in groups) so as to give them experience in learning how to use it. Through this, teachers can also develop their confidence in working in this way, especially if it is contrary to their own experiences as children or as teachers. As children become more confident and their sense of agency deepens, as in the example of Miss Shiel's class (Rogers 1969), they can be given more extensive freedom. The continual processes of communication, self-evaluation and negotiation help ensure that children and young people learn the skills to use freedom effectively.

Concentrating on personal autonomy, however, is only part of the story of developing self-governance. Although this is important, and as many of the examples in this book have shown, it is a central preoccupation of many radical free schools, there is a risk of becoming distracted with the freedom of the *individual*. As Greene (1988, p. 1) argues, when 'talk of personal freedom refers to self-dependence and self-determination; it has little to do with connectedness or being together in a community'. This concern has also been highlighted by Dewey, a principal figure within the history of democratic education. He maintained that:

> There is always a danger that increased personal independence will decrease the social capacity of the individual. In making him more self-reliant, it may make him more self-sufficient; it may lead to aloofness and indifference.
>
> (Dewey 2004, p. 42)

For schools that are interested in being communities, of creating a sense of belonging and connectedness, of operating as participative democracies, focussing on individual autonomy is not enough. In fact, it could even be said to mirror neoliberal preoccupations with self-interest and with prioritising personal needs. 'Freedom' has been heralded as a panacea for enhancing school improvement by those promoting the post-2010 models of Free Schools in UK (Gove 5 July 2012), through using it as a mechanism to achieve personal aspirations, to get ahead and to compete with others. When perceived in this way – as an 'individualistic stance' – it 'signifies a self-dependence rather than relationship; self-regarding and self-regulated behaviour rather than involvement with others' (Greene 1988, p. 7). It does not necessarily equate with being interested in the common good or with advancing social justice for all. This is the antithesis of the intentions of many of those involved in radical free schools, especially those with an explicit interest in social justice (which as has been argued throughout this book, should be all radical free schools). It is vital to consider collective interests, the good of the community as a whole, the 'will of all'. It is essential to find ways of balancing individual desires with the common good. Some decisions must be made together. This necessitates a focus on democratic or community-based decision-making – on collective self-governance.

## Mechanisms to enable effective decision-making

A community which is self-governing can been described as one in which 'in some sense or senses the actions taken or controls imposed by its governing institutions can be thought of as *originating from within that community or organization*' (Bird 2000, pp. 563–4, emphasis added). This is based on the assumption that 'each individual has a significant contribution to make and the capacity to do so' (Kensler 2010, p. 10). There has been some debate about whether 'self-governance' is the best description of the processes used within radical schools. Howard Case, pioneering Head of Epping House School UK, advocates for the phrase 'shared responsibility' (Case 1978, cited in Fielding 2013). Fielding frequently uses 'democratic fellowship' (Fielding 2013; Fielding and Moss 2011). This book uses the term 'self-governance', as it powerfully conveys the sense that children and young people are actually involved in making decisions and not simply in participating in community meetings. This coheres with models that illustrate the different levels in which children and young people may be able to participate within schools. Hart's (1992) ladder of participation has eight rungs, three of which are identified as being non-participation (including tokenism and manipulation), with the top rung being 'child initiated, shared decisions with adults'. Shier's (2001) 'pathways to participation' identified five stages, the ultimate of which is where 'children share power and responsibility for decision-making'. Fielding's (2001) 'levels of student involvement' identifies students 'working as researchers' as the most desirable level of 'genuine shared responsibility'. In this book, the phrase 'self-governance' is intended to depict these deeper levels of student participation.

Radical free schools have, since their inception, maintained that children and young people can and should be part of decision-making; that they are capable of being active and engaged members of self-governing communities. At White Lion Free School, for example, self-governance was part of the bedrock of the school. According to Wright:

> This means that the school is controlled and run by its members on an equal basis. Children, teaching staff and those who in general cater for the welfare of the children have an equal say, all decisions being taken at a General Assembly. The principle virtually abolishes the concept of 'pupils' and 'staff' as two separate entities, with separate aims and interests.
>
> (Wright 1989a, p. 105)

The use of the word 'principle' is important here. Radical free schools are driven by a set of values about the inherent qualities of children and young people, about their desires for more egalitarian relationships between 'teachers' and 'students', about their visions for the ideal school. Advocates of free schools that set up in the UK and US in the 1960s and 1970s 'sought small, intimate, and democratic communities that they could collectively control' (Miller 2002, pp. 74–5). The same motivations are still apparent today, as illustrated by a statement from the International Democratic Education Network:

> Teachers and students have an equal vote in the decisions about their learning and their social lives. . . . We believe that, in any educational setting, young people have the right: to decide individually how, when, what, where and with whom they learn; to have an equal share in the decision-making as to how their organisations – in particular their schools – are run; and which rules and sanctions, if any, are necessary.
>
> (IDEN 2018)

These statements give strong indications as to the motivations behind self-governance. It is clear as to *why* radical free schools want to offer children and young people the freedom to make choices and to be genuinely involved in decision-making. It is not clear, however, as to *how* this should happen. According to Kensler (2010, p. 1), 'this principle-based, rather than practice-based approach to designing democratic community allows for a nearly infinite array of possible organizational systems and processes within a variety of different cultures'. It is interesting to explore, therefore, how different schools and alternative learning spaces have established practices to enable self-governance as these have been 'deliberately created to enable the mass of people to act on their power to choose' (Greene 1988, p. 18).

Radical free schools have developed as independent entities, and as such, their processes for enabling community-based self-governance are all unique. Summerhill School (UK) uses whole-school meetings, ombudsmen, beddies officers and a social committee (Summerhill School 2017). The Democratic School of Hadera (Israel) uses whole-school meetings, committees, a judiciary authority and a review committee (Hecht 2011). Sudbury Valley School (US) uses whole-school meetings, a judicial committee, clerks, committees and school corporations (Sudbury Valley School 2017). Like democratic nation-states, these schools' structures and processes vary depending on context and country. The exception to this is the 'Sudbury model', which has established some specific guidelines, with a prescribed set of features, which new schools are recommended to implement regardless of location (Planning Kit, including Sudbury Valley School Handbook, available from Sudbury Valley School 2017).

Closer examination of the self-governance mechanisms of radical free schools reveal that there are distinctions in terms of how the schools have chosen to implement law-making and law-enforcing, with some combining these functions and others separating them. At Summerhill School, for example, the whole-school meeting incorporates an executive function (law-making) with a judicial one (law-enforcing); one item on the agenda might be to decide whether to introduce a new rule about bedtimes, and another item might be to deal with a complaint about a noisy student. At Sudbury Valley School, these functions are separated with the school meeting deciding on the rules and an elected judicial committee having responsibility for dealing with infringements and administering suitable punishments to law-breakers. Both of these systems have addressed the issues that arose at White Lion Free School (identified earlier) in which the responsibility for law-enforcing seemed to fall, by default, to the adults (Wright 1989b). At Summerhill School, Sudbury Valley School, the Democratic School of Hadera, Sands School and many other radical free schools, structures and processes have been deliberately created which enable children and young people to work alongside adults in law-enforcing as well as law-making.

Although the word 'democratic' can be a contentious one, with many radical free schools choosing to distance themselves from this term, it is arguably the most accurate description of schools which choose to operate as self-governing communities. The case for using this term is particularly strong when 'democracy' is perceived as much about values as about practices – values such as equality, respect and trust. Woods (2005) argues that:

> Democracy is about liberty, belonging, growth towards our true potential as human beings and a unity that suffuses diversity and difference. *Its practice is self-governance by equals.* Its core themes are creativity and the freeing of the creative social actor to seek, with others, the truths that render life and learning meaningful.
>
> (Woods 2005, p. XV, emphasis added)

These values – the values of democracy – are the ones that underpin the practices of self-governance. This is where radical free schools, which could be described as a 'microcosm of a democratic state' (Hecht 2011, p. 56), differ from their nation-state counterparts. In the former, these mini-democracies operate as 'a mode of associated living' (Dewey 2004, p. 83). They use participative democracy as a way of facilitating dialogue and of organising community life. In the latter, democracy is a political system in which 'dissent, argument, clashes of judgment, conflicts of interest and the constant formation of rival and competing factions are inevitable' (Held 2006, p. 71).

As a result, increasing numbers of people – especially young people – have become disengaged with political systems and structures and have started to look elsewhere for more effective and engaging methods for genuine political participation. Given this, there is little wonder that radical free schools frequently choose to avoid the term 'democracy'. Amos, aged 16, a student at Sands School, declares that 'country-scale democracies are just a waste of time . . . a sham'. Summerhill School states that its school meeting is 'much more orderly . . . than the UK House of Commons' (Summerhill School 2017).

In order to understand democratic schools, or radical free schools which operate democratically without actually using this terminology, it is essential to untangle the concept of operating as a democratic community from that of running a democratic nation-state. Even though 'democracy is a contested term', Ryan and Rottman (2009) argue that:

> most concepts of democracy revolve around the idea that people ought to be able to shape the institutions, culture and relationships of which

they are a part. For this to happen, at least two things must occur – people must be included in decisions that affect them and they must be able to communicate effectively with one another.

(Ryan and Rottman 2009, p. 468)

The whole-school meeting is the unifying feature of many radical free schools, and it is perhaps the most visible of all the self-governance (or democratic) practices. These meetings usually play a central role in making rules or laws, but it is important to acknowledge that not all decisions are taken by these meetings. As Holt (1972, p. 38) argues: 'we still have to decide which questions need a decision by the whole school and which ones don't. Otherwise we'll be meeting all the time'. At Summerhill School, for example, decisions about 'the business side', such as the 'hiring and firing of staff', are solely taken by adults (Summerhill School 2017). At the Democratic School of Hadera, concerns about conflictual relations between teachers and students are discussed by the Teachers Committee (Hecht 2011). Nevertheless, these whole-school meetings are commonly seen as the principal decision-making bodies, and they have considerable power. For those who have not witnessed these meetings in action, it is sometimes baffling to imagine how a group of between 50 and 100 people, some as young as 5 years old, can meaningfully engage in dialogue and collective decision-making. There is frequently the assumption that, in these contexts, democracy entails dispute, debate, argument, winners and losers. It is often imagined that decisions are made by voting. This is not always the case.

The system of voting, especially majority voting, is a key feature of many democratic processes, both within nation-states and within radical free schools. This is perhaps the simplest way of making decisions, in that a motion is proposed, those entitled to vote put their hands up (or vote secretly), and the proposal is either carried or defeated. Voting may happen quickly or it might occur only after lengthy discussion and debate. Summerhill School uses majority voting as its central method of decision-making at School Meetings. In 1962, Neill explained that:

Summerhill is a self-governing school, democratic in form. Everything connected with social, or group, life, including punishment for social offences, is settled by vote at the Saturday night General School Meeting. Each member of the teaching staff and each child, regardless of his age, has one vote.

(Neill 1962, p. 45)

This system has not changed. The Summerhill School website still states that 'each adult and child has an equal vote. Thus the youngest child has the same voting power as the Head. Not only do the children have equal power in the school meetings; they also vastly outnumber the adults' (Summerhill School 2017). Many other radical free schools utilise similar processes. Sands School uses majority voting, explaining that 'all of our rules are set by the School Meeting – we try to base them on common sense guidelines, according to the wishes of the majority' (Sands School 2018). Sudbury Valley School has formal processes for chairing meetings, and they use majority voting, though they have a distinct process for facilitating discussion, one that entails Roberts Rules of Order (Sudbury Valley School 2017).

Majority voting has been criticised, however, as 'mob rule' because it gives power to the majority to make decisions which marginalise others, without necessarily taking account of opposing information, ideas or values (Plato 1974). This is one reason why dialogue is an essential element of whole-school meetings in radical free schools, so that all voices are heard and considered. Decisions, therefore, are not about winning and losing, but about making informed and fair decisions. Nonetheless, issues might still occur. The Democratic School of Hadera uses majority voting in its school meetings, but it has also implemented an appeals process for any individual who feels that their human rights have been impinged by a community decision; investigating this is one of the roles of the review committee (Hecht 2011). Other schools have processes for enabling decisions to come back to the meeting for further consideration, especially if additional information comes to light. These are pragmatic ways to ensure that consideration is given to the concerns of the minority and to social justice.

There are radical free schools, however, which have moved away from majority voting altogether. Some schools in The Netherlands, for example, have been influenced by sociocratic decision-making methods. These were developed in the 1940s by Kees Boeke, a Dutch peace activist and educator, who established the first sociocratic school in the world (Buck and Villines 2007). He argued that majority rule is not an essential part of democracy, but rather:

> If we really wish to see the whole population united, like a big family, in which the members care for each other's welfare as much as for their own, we must set aside the quantitative principle of the right of the greatest number and find another way of organising ourselves.
>
> (Boeke, cited in Buck and Villines 2007, p. 192)

Sociocracy is based on the principle that organisations can use mutual trust to work towards the best interests of the *group as a whole* rather than simply the majority. In fact, it is sensitive to the wisdom of the *minority* (Wondering School 2018). It uses the idea of active *consent*, whereby a group or meeting identifies objections to a proposal and focuses on thinking creatively and flexibly so as to overcome these objections. In this context, consent means 'no objections'. It does not mean consensus, endorsement or unanimity. Meetings are frequently called 'circles', and there are formal processes of 'rounds' which enable everyone to contribute to the discussions and to formulating and adapting proposals. The outcome – when the process works well – is one that everyone can live with. There are no stalemates, no winners or losers.

Schools which use sociocratic decision-making methods, such as De Ruimte in The Netherlands (for children aged 4 to 18), have whole-school meetings to discuss a range of community-based issues, including those which require lengthy discussion and dialogue (De Ruimte 2018). Anyone can raise an issue or bring a proposal, just as they can in other democratic schools, but the process for reaching a decision is unique. A facilitator and a secretary will be selected. These individuals take responsibility for holding the group process. A formal procedure of using rounds – including an opening round, clarifying round, quick reaction round and consent round – will be facilitated. In every round, participants are invited to *speak in turn* in a clockwise or counter-clockwise fashion, rather than on an ad hoc or invitational basis. The spirit of the meeting is that 'we want to attune to each other' and 'we want to work together' (Buck and Villines 2007, p. 137). Some proposals may take multiple rounds, or even multiple meetings, before they can be resolved in a way that is acceptable to all. As a result, the sociocratic process could be lengthier than the use of majority voting, but arguably, the outcome will be more satisfactory for the group as a whole.

The principles of sociocracy have been used to inform the development of Roundspeak, a model for decision-making that is being used in some alternative learning spaces in the UK (Roundspeak 2018). Roundspeak is a process for making decisions which entail collective exploration in rounds on what would be best to do. Everyone brings in their own point of view, everyone is heard and a common understanding is developed. If a decision is needed, there is a procedure with a proposal, a check and an improvement of the proposal until everyone consents. Free We Grow is a new 'alternative education space which functions on democratic and humanistic principles' (Free We Grow 2018). It is based in South East London, UK. They offer an environment in which 'children's time for free-play, exploration, imagination and the pursuit of their individual or group interests is respected'. Children aged from 5 to 11 years old are able to attend the project, although most are aged from 5 to 8 years old. They are open for three days a week (the children are home educated on other days), and a community meeting is held on each of these days. A child usually chairs it. There is an allocated timekeeper. Free We Grow uses Roundspeak as a base for these meetings, although they have adapted it to include the use of hand gestures, a talking stick and occasional voting. These hand gestures signal to the chair – and to others – whether someone wants to speak, whether someone is bored or annoyed, whether someone is in agreement or disagreement and so on. A talking stick is used so that only one person speaks at a time. There are a number of different ways in which decisions are made during the meeting. A simple show of hands (majority vote) determines, for example, whether lunch will be eaten inside or outside (everyone eats together). Other decisions are made through consent. Decisions on whether, for example, to allow particular individuals to visit the school or offer workshops are made through 'rounds', where each person can consent or object. An objection implies there are specific reasons for the person not to agree or fully agree to a proposal, and it opens up discussion and the possibility of seeing things through other perspectives. These views are then used to refine the proposals. Final decisions, including the adoption of new rules, are made by the consent of everyone in the meeting. Any new rules are written down in a rule book. Given that the meeting takes place every day, it is easy to ensure that all issues are addressed quickly, and with everyone present.

## What is an appropriate age to start involving children and young people in decision-making?

It seems self-evident that when children and young people have a freedom to choose, whether on an individual basis (micro level) or as part of collective self-governance (macro level), there are likely to be associated risks. Some of the children at Summerhill School and at Free We Grow are 5 years old. Some at Sudbury Valley and the Democratic School of Hadera are only 4. The mere idea of involving children in decision-making has been heavily criticised by some involved with conventional education. In 2010, the Teachers' Union (NASUWT)'s general secretary in the UK, Chris Keates, argued that: 'Children are not small adults. They are in schools to learn, not to teach or manage the school' (cited in Williams 2010). Critics argue that 'when a teacher grants pupils responsibility for their own learning, they also grant them responsibility for their own failure' (Peal 2014, p. 193). These criticisms lead to essential but challenging questions as to whether children and young people are competent to make good use of freedom, and if so, whether this is dependent on their age.

The principle of offering responsible freedom in education necessitates a willingness to allow the child, young person or adult to make a poor choice, to make a *mistake*. This might be a small mistake, such as wishing that s/he had written a story in a different way; this is something that can be reflected on, learned from and the learning embedded into future decision-making. This is a valuable mistake, and one in which the student can usually cope with the consequences (disappointment, frustration, anger at self or others). The importance of being able to make mistakes has been highlighted by those involved with radical free schools (see Chapter Three). However, some choices – possibly named as mistakes – have more far-reaching consequences. This might be, for example, the decision to not attend any lessons for a whole term or a whole year, the decision not to take any formal qualifications throughout schooling, the decision to play computer games rather than attend mealtimes. Are there occasions when decisions are too big for a child and thus need to be made for them? Are students being encouraged to make uninformed decisions when they cannot foresee the long-term consequences of decisions which they make today? This is the premise on which conventional education is built – a premise which says that curriculum, syllabus, teaching methods and assessment regimes must be standardised for all children, so that children (and also, by implication, parents) do not have to face the consequences of making poor decisions. This stance posits that children (and their parents) cannot be trusted to make decisions, and therefore, decisions need to be made on their behalf. This paternalistic position is not one that those who advocate giving students 'freedom to choose' would accept. By advocating a more liberatory way of educating, teachers and educators take the position that children, young people and adults *can* be trusted, and moreover, that it serves the long-term interests of education to offer them this freedom.

It is reasonable to accept, as has been indicated by students in radical free schools, that freedom is 'something you need to grow into' (Pernille, age 15, Hellerup School). Freedom shock appears to be real (Hecht 2011). As Goodlad (1996, p. 105) argues, 'we are not born knowing the art of conversation that is central to the moral art of democracy'. Radical free schools, therefore, need to pay attention to the competencies of children and young people, and must find ways of supporting them to develop the attitudes and skills necessary to make effective use of their freedom. As has already been discussed in this chapter, this might include offering a narrower range of choices until a child is more confident and then gradually extending the options available to them. An example of this has been given in relation to Hellerup School where, as Katrine, a 15-year-old student, explained: 'you work a lot more in your class when you're younger but when you get older you get more freedom to go out and work yourself or work in a group' (see Chapter Three).

There is still an issue to face, nonetheless, and this relates to the age at which children are able to use their agency to enact their freedom. This dilemma is outlined by Cate, a teacher in a small democratic school in Australia:

> Freedom becomes a problem for us in that they have to have certain skills to go up to high school *before they've got the maturity* . . . a 17-year-old knowing they have to do an exam, they've got the maturity to do it . . . but an 11-year or 12-year-old doesn't have that maturity themselves.

> (IDEC Group Interview 2016)

Similarly, Eric, a teacher in Germany, argues that: 'If you are 16 years old, maybe your responsibility for your own life is different from when you're six years old' (IDEC Group Interview 2016). It would be unreasonable to suggest that all children, of all ages, are able to manage responsible freedom in the way that adults can. Indeed, there are many examples of when *adults* struggle when offered freedom (Freire 1970; hooks 1994; Hope 2018). Bessant (2014), however, posits that suggestions that children are *incapable* of managing freedom are based on essentialist thinking that perceives children as deficient. She suggests that this view routinely denies children opportunities to practice exercising good judgment. Instead, she proposes the use of the Capability Approach, arguing that 'people age differently in diverse social contexts and develop capacities at different times and often not in linear progressive ways' (Bessant 2014, p. 151). Using this approach would mean that 'students be supported to make informed choices' and that 'in exercising such freedom, they would learn of the available alternatives, the consequences of each and the paths to achieve them' (Bessant 2014, p. 145). This implies that children's ability to use freedom is not necessarily age-specific, but rather, is a more personalised process. Where one child might be able to think through the consequences of decisions, others may not. Through this lens, offering freedom to students is a principled position, the enactment of which might differ on a student-by-student and context-by-context basis. Some 5-year-olds might feel able to participate fully in whole-school meetings, but some 15-year-olds might not. Radical free schools have the flexibility within their structures and processes to allow for this.

## Summary

Freedom can be conceptualised in many ways, but as this chapter has argued, experiencing a genuine 'freedom to choose' is essential for students within radical free schools. This might be seen as an overarching category which envelops many other types of freedom, including freedom to create, freedom to be, freedom to think, freedom to become, freedom to be accepted, freedom to explore, freedom to develop and freedom to learn.

Freedom to choose is inextricably intertwined with self-governance, both on a micro level (development of personal autonomy and self-determination) and on a macro level (involvement in whole-school decision-making). Both of these are important, though as has been argued, there are inherent dangers with offering the former without paying attention to the latter. The former is necessary but not sufficient. Advancing personal autonomy at the expense of community-building can inadvertently promote individualism, and for schools that value connectedness, belongingness and social justice, this is clearly problematic.

Many radical free schools have a deep commitment to operating as self-governing communities, as participative democracies (even if they do not use this phrase). Through investigating the mechanisms that many of these schools use in practice, it is apparent that there is not a 'best model' to use. Some separate legislative and judicial functions; others do not. Some use majority voting; others use sociocratic methods or Roundspeak. They have different procedures for deciding what is taken to a whole-school meeting and what is dealt with elsewhere. These nuances, though interesting, are not the central issue. What connects these schools is their commitment to democratic values – to equality, respect, valuing the contribution of each person, finding ways of enabling each individual to participate and be taken seriously and having non-hierarchical relationships between children and adults. These are the essential features of radical free schools. These values underpin all structures and processes. Through holding true to these values, conditions have then been 'deliberately created to enable the mass of people to act on their power to choose' (Greene 1988, p. 18). These structures and processes are what enable children and young people to genuinely experience a freedom to choose.

## References

Berlin, I. 1969/2007. "Two Concepts of Liberty (1969)." In *Freedom: A Philosophical Anthology*, edited by I. Carter, M.H. Kramer and H. Steiner. Oxford: Blackwell Publishing.

Bessant, J. 2014. "A Dangerous Idea? Freedom, Children and the Capability Approach to Education." *Critical Studies in Education* 55 (2):138–53.

Bird, C. 2000. "The Possibility of Self-Government." *The American Political Science Review* 94 (3):563–77.

Boud, D. 1988. "Moving Towards Autonomy." In *Developing Student Autonomy in Learning: 2nd Ed*, edited by D. Boud. London: Kogan Page Ltd.

Buck, J., and S. Villines. 2007. *We the People: Consenting to a Deeper Democracy*. Washington: Sociocracy.Info.

Carter, I., M.H. Kramer, and H. Steiner. 2007. *Freedom: A Philosophical Anthology*. Oxford: Blackwell Publishing.

Case, H. 1978. *Loving Us: A New Way of Education*. Privately published [copy held by London University Institute of Education Library, Classmark zz SA6390].

*De Ruimte*. 2018. "Home Page." Available at: https://deruimtesoest.nl/.

Dewey, J. 2004. *Democracy and Education*. New York: Dover Publications (originally published 1916).

Dworkin, G. 2007. "The Theory and Practice of Autonomy (1988)." In *Freedom: A Philosophical Anthology*, edited by I. Carter, M.H. Kramer and H. Steiner. Oxford: Blackwell Publishing.

Fielding, M. 2001. "Students as Radical Agents of Change." *Journal of Educational Change* 2:123–41.

Fielding, M. 2013. "Whole School Meetings and the Development of Radical Democratic Community." *Studies in Philosophy and Education* 32:123–40.

Fielding, M., and P. Moss. 2011. *Radical Education and the Common School: A Democratic Alternative*. Oxon: Routledge.

Free We Grow. "Home Page." Accessed 17/06/18. http://freewegrow.co.uk/.

*Freedom to Learn Project*. 2017. "Freedom to Learn Manifesto." Accessed 29/11/17.

Freire, P. 1970. *Pedagogy of the Oppressed*. London: Penguin Books.

Goodlad, J.I. 1996. "Democracy, Education and Community." In *Democracy, Education and the Schools*, edited by R. Soder. San Francisco: Jossey-Bass Publishers.

Gove, M. 5 July 2012. "Speech on FASNA's first twenty years – pioneers of excellence." In *Freedom and Autonomy for Schools National Association Conference*, London.

Greene, M. 1988. *The Dialectic of Freedom*. New York: Teachers College Press.

Hart, R. 1992. *Children's Participation: From Tokenism to Citizenship, Innocenti Essays No 4*. Florence: UNICEF.

Hecht, Y. 2011. *Democratic Education: A Beginning of a Story*. New York: Alternative Education Resource Organization.

Held, D. 2006. *Models of Democracy (3rd Ed)*. Cambridge: Polity Press.

Holt, J. 1972. *Freedom and Beyond*. New York: E.P. Dutton and Company Inc.

hooks, b. 1994. *Teaching to Trangress: Education as the Practice of Freedom*. Oxon: Routledge.

Hope, M.A. 2018. "Democratic Education in Universities: Pushing at the Boundaries." *Other Education: The Journal of Educational Alternatives* 7 (1):42–5.

IDEN. 2018. "What Is Democratic Education?" *International Democratic Education Network*. Accessed 15/03/18. Available at: www.idenetwork.org/index.php/about/what-is-democratic-education.

Kensler, L.A.W. 2010. "Designing Democratic Community." *International Journal of Urban Education Leadership* 4 (1):1–21.

Miller, R. 2002. *Free Schools, Free People: Education and Democracy After the 1960s*. Albany: State University of New York Press.

Montgomery, C., and M.A. Hope. 2016. "Thinking the Yet to Be Thought: Envisioning Autonomous and Alternative Pedagogies for Socially Just Education." *FORUM: For Promoting 3–19 Comprehensive Education* 58: 307–314.

Morrison, K.A. 2008. "Democratic Classrooms: Promises and Challenges of Student Voice and Choice, Part One." *Educational Horizons* 87 (1):50–60.

Neill, A.S. 1962. *Summerhill: A Radical Approach to Education.* London: Victor Gollancz Ltd.

Peal, R. 2014. *Progressively Worse: The Burden of Bad Ideas in British Schools.* London: Civitas.

Plato. 1974. *The Republic: 2nd Edition (translated by Lee, D.).* Harmondsworth: Penguin Books.

Rogers, C. 1969. *Freedom to Learn.* Ohio: Charles E. Merrill Publishing Company.

Rogers, C. 1980. *A Way of Being.* Boston: Houghton Mifflin Company.

Roundspeak. "Roundspeak Effective Meetings." Accessed 15/03/18. http://www.roundspeak-meetings.com/.

Ryan, J., and C. Rottman. 2009. "Struggling for Democracy: Administrative Communication in a Diverse School Context." *Educational Management Administration & Leadership* 37:473–96.

*Sands School.* 2018. "Home Page." Accessed 13/02/18. Available at: www.sandsschool.co.uk/.

Shier, H. 2001. "Pathways to Participation: Openings, Opportunities and Obligations." *Children & Society* 15:107–17.

*Sudbury Valley School.* 2017. "Home Page." Accessed 30/11/17. Available at: www.sudburyvalley.org/01_abou_01.html.

*Summerhill School.* 2017. "Home Page." Accessed 30/11/17. Available at: www.summerhillschool.co.uk/.

Van Parijs, P. 1995/2007. "Real Freedom for All (1995)." In *Freedom: A Philosophical Anthology*, edited by I. Carter, M.H. Kramer and H. Steiner. Oxford: Blackwell Publishing.

Williams, R. 2010. "Union say pupils on interview panels are humiliating teachers." In *The Guardian.*

*Wondering School.* 2018. "Sociocracy in Schools [Film]." Accessed 15/03/18. Available at: www.wonderingschool.org/videos/.

Woods, P.A. 2005. *Democratic Leadership in Education.* London: Sage Publications.

Wright, N. 1989a. *Assessing Radical Education.* Milton Keynes: Open University Press.

Wright, N. 1989b. *Free School: The White Lion Experience.* Leicestershire: Libertarian Education.

# 6 The case for freedom
## A call to action

### Introduction

> Won't you help to sing
> These songs of freedom?
> 'Cause all I ever have
> Redemption songs
>
> (Bob Marley 1980)

Freedom is under threat. In recent years, it has been identified as a potential tool for 'driving up standards' in education, as a weapon for schools to use in a competitive neoliberal marketplace. Many of the advocates for offering freedom in education – or more specifically, for offering freedom to students – have distanced themselves from the concept. They have started to use terms such as 'alternative' or 'innovative' as descriptors and have subtly dropped the word 'free'. The language of 'freedom' and 'autonomy' has become common parlance for conservatives and traditionalists and for those with a market-orientated agenda, and as a result, the concept has become distorted.

This book emanates from the position that the current education system, in the UK and beyond, is deeply flawed, even broken. Despite continued efforts by successive governments, inequalities in education continue to increase (Baker et al. 2004). Rates of formal and informal exclusion are high, with particular social groups being disproportionately affected (Parsons 2005; Department for Education 2013). Teachers are leaving the profession in droves (Boffey 2015). Students finish school without the skills and qualifications that employers expect (Youth Employment UK 2017). Even Michael Gove, Education Secretary in the UK (2010–2014), argued that: 'We need nothing short of radical, whole-scale reform' (Gove 20 June 2011). Within this context, change is needed, and as Reay (2012, p. 589) has posited, 'Tinkering with an unjust educational system is not going to transform it into a just system'. This calls for *radical* action. This chapter makes the case, building on the arguments presented in the preceding chapters, that reclaiming freedom in education is key to this process.

This chapter starts by exploring some of the challenges encountered by those who strive to offer freedom in education – challenges for teachers, students and schools in themselves. This is followed by discussion on what schools (and other educators) might need to do in order to establish and maintain freedom in education. This section contains a note of caution, as there is no simple blueprint or single model to emulate, although, as this section argues, there are a number of unifying common themes. Finally, with the use of three propositions, the case is presented as to *why* freedom matters. This chapter – and the book – ends with a call to action about building communities of activists –teachers, parents, students, school leaders, of informal educators – who can collectively 'sing these songs of freedom'.

## Confronting the challenges of offering freedom in education

### *Challenges for teachers*

For teachers, the experiences of being involved in schools that are committed to freedom can be challenging. Even getting to be a teacher at some of these radical free schools can be a hurdle. Many do not pay competitive salaries or even any salaries at all. Some recruit staff through the mechanism of 'voting in' at school-wide meetings, and this system also means that staff can be 'voted out' again. Teachers usually do not have the same job descriptions as teachers in other schools, and in some cases, 'teaching' might not even be part of the role. In these schools, teachers and students 'become jointly responsible for a process in which all grow . . . here, no one teaches another, nor is anyone self-taught' (Freire 1970, p. 61). For teachers, this requires a completely different way of being.

The vast majority of teachers, in radical schools and elsewhere, have not personally been educated in schools, colleges or universities which offer freedom. Emilie, an educator from Brazil, alludes to this point by stating that 'the biggest challenge for us is that *we are adults*, so we need to . . . start imagining and creating ways for how to give freedom to the kids'. This is not easy or simple, as stories from Summerhill, Sudbury Valley and the Democratic School of Hadera attest (see Chapter Three). In relation to Sudbury Valley, Greenberg (1987, p. 20) says,

> We get a lot of people writing to the school asking to be hired as teachers. Many of them tell us at length how much they have to "give" to

students. People like that don't do too well at the school. What's important to us is what the students want to take, not what the teachers want to give. That's hard for a lot of professional teachers to grasp.

Even if teachers – or other staff – are willing to experiment with their roles and deliberately develop more egalitarian and dialogic relationships with students, there is a further challenge as to how *hands-off or hands-on* they should be in terms of sharing knowledge and offering opinions, activities or lessons. Piotr, an educator from Poland, poses some interesting questions: 'can adults and other people in the community share their perspective . . . and their way of thinking what is right and what is wrong with children? And if that is happening, is that taking a freedom away from them?' He goes on to explain, using an example, 'if I love maths and I'm going to share my love for maths, does it mean I'm taking a freedom away from the child because s/he will be influenced and maybe start to do maths too?' (IDEC Group Interview 2016). This dilemma is complicated further when there is an overt commitment to social justice, such as in Mississippi Freedom Schools or in Pride School Atlanta (see Chapter Four). Here, teachers might have knowledge and information that they believe is vital to the 'freedom struggle', and they have to then make complex decisions about when to be proactive in offering 'lessons' and sharing 'knowledge' and when to stand back and enable students to self-direct their own individual learning journeys.

These tensions are not easily resolved. The notion of freedom can be conceptualised differently. Wei-Ting, a 15-year-old student in a democratic school in Taiwan, believes that 'it's pretty related to culture . . . freedom might be pretty different in different countries because of their culture'. Lina from Lithuania agrees, stating that 'it's socially constructed, that why it means so many different things for different people' (IDEC Group Interview 2016). These contrasting interpretations of freedom mean that teachers and educators might hold divergent perspectives on what freedom looks like in theory and in practice. Some radical free schools – or some teachers with them – might argue that students must always be in control, that offering freedom means entirely trusting that students can decide what they want to engage with and learn. For schools that are committed to a social justice agenda, this position could seem ill judged as it runs the risk of placing an '*excessive* emphasis on freedom at the expense of other educational, cultural and even psychological values' (Miller 2002, p. 32, emphasis in original). In order to play a role in advancing social justice, radical free schools need to find the balance between offering freedom and challenging social inequalities.

## Challenges for students

Many of the stories shared throughout this book demonstrate that when – if – students start to trust the freedom that they have in these radical free schools, the consequences can be powerful. Mia, aged 14, from Hellerup School, said that 'you learn to take care of yourself and be responsible for what you learn'. In this quote, she is referring to a personal level of responsibility (linking with the micro level of freedom), but Amos, aged 16, a student at Sands School, articulates this in relation to school-wide decisions (macro level). He said: 'they can take serious decisions very seriously'. Kativa, an educator from India, argued that: 'people think we can be undisciplined, we can be irresponsible, but actually this is the other way round . . . when you get freedom you have to be *more* responsible and self-disciplined' (IDEC Group Interview 2016).

It is important to recognise, nonetheless, that students do not always adjust easily to their new-found freedom. 'Freedom shock' (Hecht 2011) appears to be real and widespread, with many schools and educators reporting on this. Students like Clare, aged 15, at Sands School, explain that they had 'taken advantage of the freedom a lot' by not attending lessons or proactively engaging in school meetings. Mathilda, a 15-year-old student at Hellerup School, shares a story of someone who wanted more structure, more direction and 'a tighter schedule and tighter rules' (see Chapter Three). This is perhaps to be expected. As Holt (1972, p. 78) argues: 'If we make this offer of freedom, choice, self-direction to students who have spent much time in traditional schools, most of them will not trust us or believe us. Given their experience, they are quite right not to'. This concurs with arguments from Macmurray (1949) and Rogers (1980, p. 273), the latter stating that 'Students have been "conned" for so long that a teacher who is real with them is usually seen for a time as simply exhibiting a new brand of phoniness'. This does not just apply to schools. Students in universities can be equally nervous about being offered freedom, with many of them preferring to fall back on more familiar teacher-directed approaches to learning (Hope 2018; hooks 1994).

Teachers are able to support students to adjust to using their freedom effectively; to find ways to enact their 'real freedom', their agency (Van Parijs 1995/2007). Methods for doing so were discussed in Chapter Four, as they form a crucial part of enabling students to be able to exercise the 'freedom to choose'. They include gradually widening the number of choices available so as to support students to start to trust themselves with making choices, supporting students to reflect on their own preferred ways of learning, being willing to encourage students to make 'mistakes', and developing mechanisms for involving students in collective decision-making.

*Challenges for schools*

Schools do not operate in isolation, and in many neoliberal education 'markets', there are in-built elements of competition in education system. This affects schools as well as individual students. This can present a considerable challenge for schools that wish to operate differently and which hold a contrasting set of values to those held by other schools.

In Denmark, there is an accountability system that means that Hellerup School is compared, in terms of its academic results, with other schools in the area. Even if teachers at the school want to prioritise other aspects of schooling, such as personal and social development or the development of self-confidence, they feel a pressure to make sure that the students perform well in standardised tests (Hope 2017). This affects the freedom that they – the school – are able to offer. The school's own sense of agency (real freedom) is thus compromised. Privately funded schools, such as Summerhill, Sands School and Sudbury Valley School, have more freedom in this respect, but they still encounter expectations from parents. Simone from the US alludes to this issue: 'the parents . . . want something different for their own children but yet when it looks different they question whether or not their children will be successful. It's a fear' (IDEC Group Interview 2016). In addition, the students can exert pressure. At the Democratic School of Hadera, Hecht (2011) describes how some children find themselves wanting to prove that they can work harder and achieve *more* than they had previously in other schools. He attributes this to 'freedom shock' but explains that it can still be challenging for schools to address.

In the light of these pressures – from accountability regimes, parents and students – it can be hard for schools to hold firm to their values and to resist the pressure to steer students in particular directions. The schools must be sufficiently robust to ensure that they can counter any criticisms. For some, this requires brave and bold leadership.

## How can freedom be established and maintained?: unifying themes

Different cultures have developed within radical free schools. All schools are unique. The political, geographical, social, economic and educational environments in which they are based are all quite distinct. As a result, they face different challenges and evolve in their own ways (as demonstrated by the case studies throughout this book). There is no one-size-fits-all blueprint for how schools and other education settings should offer freedom. There are, nonetheless, some common themes that are expedient for *all* schools and learning spaces in *all* contexts to consider.

This is not just relevant to radical free schools. All schools, and indeed other educational establishments, have the capacity to be 'freedom-based', to have a 'pedagogy of freedom' (Freire 2001) or an 'orientation towards freedom' (Säfström and Biesta 2011). This challenges the dominant assumption that educational freedom can only be offered in alternative schools, those in the independent sector, those that are fee-paying. It is frequently assumed that state-funded mainstream schools are too constrained and, thus, do not have the luxury of focussing on these matters. This is a mistake. Although independent schools might have more freedom and thus more autonomy to make bold decisions on structures, processes, curriculum and pedagogy, there are numerous examples of state-funded mainstream schools – and teachers within them – that have done so. These include the original free schools in the 1960s and 1970s in the UK, Countesthorpe College and St George-in-the-East (UK), Hellerup School (Denmark) and many of the schools-within-schools (SWS) models (initially developed in the US) (Wallace 2009). It could, of course, also include the post-2010 Academies and Free Schools in the UK, though research evidence suggests that this is rare (Wiborg et al. 2018).

It is worth remembering, in addition, that education does not just take place in schools. It is both 'lifewide' and 'lifelong' (OECD 2007). It takes place in nurseries, schools, colleges and universities. It includes youth and community work. It can be informal or formal. It might include home education. It could be work-based. It might include apprenticeships or mentoring schemes. It might be entirely personal and self-directed. There is a wide range of ways in which learning can take place. All of these can utilise freedom. The arguments in this book are not restricted to schools. Freedom in education can and does take place anywhere.

There are three central ways, it is suggested here, in which freedom can be established and maintained within education. These are deliberately brief as they act as summaries of much of what has already been explored within this book. These are:

a   Developing more egalitarian and democratic structures, practices and processes
b   Utilising liberating pedagogies and reforming curricula to enable personalised learning and the acknowledgement of multiple perspectives and outlooks
c   Creating smaller communities in which all are known and can belong

## Developing more egalitarian and democratic structures, practices and processes

Democratisation is important. This means that structures and processes need to be developed which align with the *values* of democracy; with equality, trust, respect and belonging. Schools do not necessarily have to describe themselves as democratic as such, but the values of democracy are integral to all education which wants to enhance freedom for students. These influence decision-making processes, policies, pedagogies, curricula, relationships between staff and student and decisions on age mixing. As Lynch and Baker argue:

> At the level of teacher – student relationships, it involves substituting dialogue for dominance, cooperation and collegiality for hierarchy, and active learning and problem solving for passivity . . . At the level of school and college organization, it involves institutionalizing and resourcing democratic structures such as student and parent/community councils that exercise real authority and responsibility. It also requires initiating new systems of dialogue with students, teachers, parents and local communities.
>
> (Lynch and Baker 2005, p. 149)

A commitment to developing egalitarian and democratic ways of working inevitably leads to questions about how decisions are made within schools, and in particular, who is involved in making which decisions. Education which is based on freedom does not necessarily equate with the need to have whole-school meetings or to function as participative democracies, but as has been explored in Chapter Five, offering a real 'freedom to choose' has implications for collective, as well as individual, self-governance. All schools and other educational establishments need to consider how they can develop collective decision-making processes which are congruent with the aims and intentions of the organisation.

## *Utilising liberating pedagogies and reforming curricula to enable personalised learning and the acknowledgement of multiple perspectives and outlooks*

Radically changing curricula and pedagogies is essential within all schools that want to offer a liberating experience. Not only do they need to be more flexible and responsible to align with the interests of students, but they also need to take account of social justice. Traditional curricula have been criticised for presenting a partial and one-sided view of history and of society. This sanitised curriculum serves the interests of those in positions of power and privilege and operates as a form of cultural reproduction (see Chapter Four). Similarly, traditional pedagogy which sees the teacher as 'expert' and does not encourage challenge or critical thinking exacerbates these issues as students are not able to deeply engage with the material that is presented to them. This way of teaching is exemplified in *Harry Potter and the Order of the Phoenix*, where the dictatorial Professor Umbridge reprimands a student, arguing 'I am here to teach you using a Ministry-approved method that does not include inviting students to give their opinions on matters about which they understand very little' (Rowling 2003, p. 284). Within schools that strive to offer a greater degree of freedom, changing the nature of the teacher-student relationship is of central importance. Teachers become 'facilitators' (Rogers 1980) or 'teacher-students with student-teachers' (Freire 1970). They use pedagogies which encourage and enable critical engagement and the questioning of knowledge. The cases of the Mississippi Freedom Schools and Pride School Atlanta are particularly strong examples of the way in which schools can radically alter curricula and pedagogies in order to intertwine an orientation towards social justice with critical and liberatory pedagogies.

## Creating smaller communities in which all are known and can belong

A further issue relates to school size (Hope 2012b). Although it has not been explicitly highlighted, all of the schools and alternative learning spaces used as case studies in this book are small (see Chapter One for breakdown of all cases and the numbers of students in attendance). The largest of these has approximately 660 students and the smallest has less than a dozen. This is not a coincidence. As E.F. Schumacher, author of *Small is Beautiful*, posited: 'people can be themselves only in small comprehensible groups' (Schumacher 1993, p. 57). There is growing recognition that, in relation to schools, 'Smallness is a prerequisite for the climate and culture that we need to develop the habits of heart and mind essential to a democracy' (Meier 1996, p. 12). For many schools, this presents problems as there is a tendency in some countries to create mega-schools that benefit from economies of scale. In recent years, however, creative approaches of developing 'schools-within-schools' (SWS) have been used to break down larger schools into smaller mini-schools, all with their own unique identities (Wallace 2009). Within these mini-schools, which exhibit the 'characteristics of smallness' (Haimendorf and Kestner 2009, p. 12), students have been able to develop a strong sense of belonging, and democratic structures and processes have been able to be employed. Large schools, therefore, are not inherently prevented from being democratic and from offering freedom.

Creating small, intimate communities of learners – of children, young people and adults – is essential in terms of facilitating belonging. Belongingness is essential for all children, young people and adults (Hope 2012c). It is also critical in order to enable that everyone feels that they have freedom and a real sense of agency to use this in practice.

**Why does freedom matter anyway? three propositions**

Schools with a commitment to freedom sometimes appear to take for granted that freedom is, in itself, a good thing. In fact, advocates of the 800 or so 'original free schools' in the US have been criticised for celebrating freedom 'excessively' (Miller 2002, p. 174). Given this, and given the way that freedom has been appropriated for other ends, it is crucial that schools that are committed to freedom are able to be clear and convincing about why offering freedom is important. Three propositions are offered here, all of which include references to published evidence that reinforces their credibility. The first relates to human rights, the second to the outcomes of education and the third to improved school environments.

> Proposition 1: International Human Rights Conventions stipulate that all children and young people have the right to be heard and to be able to influence their own education.

There is a moral imperative to offer freedom within education. Put simply, it is the 'right thing to do'. This is a powerful argument which might seem instinctive to some advocates of freedom, but it can also be reinforced with reference to international human rights conventions. The UN Convention on the Rights of the Child (United Nations 1989) has been signed by 195 countries, meaning that it is the most widely ratified human rights treaty in history. Article 12 outlines that 'States Parties shall assure to the child who is capable of forming his or her own views the right to express those views freely in all matters affecting the child'. Article 13 states that 'the child shall have the right to freedom of expression'. Article 14 emphasises that states should 'respect the right of the child to freedom of thought, conscience and religion'. Article 29 specifies that 'the education of the child shall be directed to . . . the development of the child's personality, talents and mental and physical abilities to their fullest potential'. The structures, processes and pedagogies of radical free schools are clearly aligned with these principles in that they place great emphasis on offering freedom of speech, thought, association and choice. By offering such a high degree of personalised learning and freedom, they also demonstrate that they offer educational opportunities which are directed towards each child's personality, talents and abilities. The stories of Sands School, Summerhill School, Sudbury Valley School, Hellerup School and the Democratic School of Hadera (see Chapter Three) are all powerful illustrations of how these rights have been enacted in practice.

The Convention also makes explicit links with a social justice agenda, stating that rights are available 'without discrimination of any kind, irrespective of the child's or his or her parent's or legal guardian's race, colour, sex, language, religion, political or other opinion, national, ethnic or social origin, property, disability, birth or other status' (Article 2). This strengthens the argument, made throughout this book, that freedom needs to be intertwined with an overt commitment to social justice. The examples of the Mississippi Freedom Schools, CDF Freedom Schools and Pride School Atlanta (see Chapter Four) all show how curriculum and pedagogy can be creatively developed to achieve these ends.

It is important to note that the UN Convention on the Rights of the Child specifically refers to *rights*. These are not *gifts* bestowed on children and young people who live in certain countries or who behave in particular ways. They should not be dependent on a nation's economic resources or on the political position of governments. They are *universal rights*, and as such, they are powerful justifications which can be utilised by those committed to freedom within education. All children, in all schools, in all countries, have an entitlement to these rights. Schools which offer freedom are clearly driven, implicitly and explicitly, by a commitment to these rights.

Proposition 2: Schools which are underpinned by a commitment to freedom have improved educational outcomes.

There is extensive evidence that many students who experience freedom in schools do well, particularly in relation to three educational outcomes: 1) the development of autonomy, 2) positive engagement in 'learning' and 3) active citizenship. There is a word of caution here. Gathering data about educational outcomes is notoriously difficult, and this is exacerbated by the fact that many radical free schools hold a counter-narrative as to the purpose of education and can thus be resistant to using 'outcome-based' measures of effectiveness. Nonetheless, much of the existing evidence is persuasive in demonstrating that these types of school environment have a positive impact on educational outcomes.

First, offering freedom in schools appears to have a powerful influence on the development of autonomy (as demonstrated in Chapter Five). It is widely accepted that increasing student autonomy is desirable; indeed, it has been described as 'a goal of education' (Boud 1988, p. 17). Students within education where they have freedom frequently become more self-directed, self-reliant and autonomous (Hope 2010; Rogers 1980; Aspy and Roebuck 1974; Cornelius-White 2007; Davies, Williams and Yamashita 2005b). These are significant outcomes. They are essential skills for all students, and equally importantly, for individuals who are to become effective citizens within democratic nations. Students in many of the schools discussed in Chapters Three, Four and Five have described how their experiences in radical free schools have supported them to become more responsible, self-directed and autonomous. In Chapter Three, Clare from Sands School said, 'Oh my god, I rule my own life at the moment'. Having this level of responsibility – emanating from freedom – is not always straightforward, as discussed earlier and exemplified by the phrases 'freedom shock' and 'drunk on freedom' (Hecht 2011). Nonetheless, when students are able to embrace their freedom and use it effectively, it appears to have a significant impact on the development of personal and group-based autonomy. This is important.

Second, students in freer environments have been shown to be more engaged in 'learning' (Hope 2010; OECD 2007; Davies, Williams and Yamashita 2005b). Needless to say, the definition of 'learning' is important here, as the infamous case of Summerhill School's battle with Ofsted[1] powerfully demonstrates (for details, see Vaughan 2006). 'Learning' should not be conflated with 'lessons' as learning in free schools can take place anywhere, at any time, in any way. When students are offered freedom, and are thus able to make choices about when, how and what to learn, their engagement increases. This engagement might relate to so-called soft skills (such as communication, self-esteem, teamwork, conflict management), but evidence suggests that it could link with more measurable 'academic' learning. Clare at Sands School, for example, stated that 'It would be really great if I left with decent marks, which I will definitely try my hardest for'. It is important, however, to ensure that there is no collusion with a hierarchy between 'soft' and 'hard' outcomes. As the children and young people at Pride School Atlanta eloquently demonstrated (in Chapter Four), their ability to engage meaningfully in academic learning was inextricably linked with their levels of safety, peer acceptance and personal self-confidence. As Dylan explained, 'Because like I don't worry about what's going to happen to me here all the time. so instead of my mind being filled with that *it has space for work*'. This is vital. Being able to engage in learning – in all learning – is a crucial element of education, and offering freedom within schools appears to have a notable influence on this ability.

Third, the development of 'citizenship skills' for students is vastly aided by being participants within functioning self-governing communities and mini-democracies (Hope 2012a; Maitles and Deuchar 2006; Maitles and Gilchrist 2006; Coffield and Williamson 2011). It is widely acknowledged that an important function of all schools is to teach students about the rights and responsibilities of citizenship and to prepare them for being active and constructive citizens within their local, national and international contexts. There has been a long-standing debate, nonetheless, as to the most effective ways to acquire these skills. Bernard Crick, architect of Britain's first formalised 'citizenship curriculum', argued that 'Citizenship by prescription, order, rote, grid or check-list is not true citizenship at all. The name of the game is, of course, not citizenship *teaching* but citizenship *learning*' (Crick 2007, p. 242, emphasis added). Experiential learning (learning by doing) – which is the way that students in free schools usually learn about citizenship – offers a far more productive way for students to engage at a deep level. Through having responsible freedom and being accountable for the impact of their own actions on others, they learn to be active and constructive members of communities (see Chapter Five). This is not always easy for students, as some of the stories in this book demonstrate, but it is nonetheless invaluable. Students in these self-governing communities clearly demonstrate a deep commitment to themselves, each other and the school as a whole (Hope 2010). Given the increasing global concerns about the alienation of children and young people from political processes and from communities, this is highly significant.

> Proposition 3: School environments are more positive within freer schools, enabling students to be happier and more constructive, and teachers to be non-hierarchical and less disciplinarian.

Schools which are underpinned by freedom, whether or not they describe themselves as 'democratic', appear to create happier and more constructive environments for all. There is considerable evidence – much of it gathered in conventional schools – that developing environments in which students can meaningfully participate in school life and in decision-making results in improved relationships between students, an improved school environment, more adherence to school rules, a reduction in conflict between staff and students and a greater degree of care among all school members (Baginsky and Hannam 1999; Gold and Gold 1998; Davies, Williams, and Yamashita 2005a). Given the challenges that many schools face in terms of student behaviour and discipline issues, these outcomes are crucial.

In schools which explicitly describe themselves as 'democratic' and embed the values of democracy into all structures and processes, the impact on the school environment is even more striking. Harber (1996) suggests that there are four reasons for this: 1) rules are better kept by staff and students if democratically agreed on in the first place; 2) communications in the schools are improved; 3) there is an increased sense of responsibility as staff and pupils have more control over their own organisation, overcoming the 'them and us' alienation in most schools; 4) decision-making is improved as a range of internal and external interests and opinions is considered.

Students at Sands School described their previous experiences of school as being a 'big battle' characterised by a 'teachers-versus-students mindset', and students at Hellerup School said they had felt 'like you're almost like trapped in a box' (see Chapter Three). Students at Pride School Atlanta explained how they had woken up scared and afraid that they would be 'bullied and beat up' (see Chapter Four). Students' experiences in radical free schools were completely different from these. In these new environments, they enjoyed being at school, they had fun, they got on well with their teachers, they meaningfully participated in learning and they took part in making decisions. In addition, teachers reported feeling a sense of freedom, especially in Pride School Atlanta, where staff could be themselves and tell the 'whole story' of the curriculum. The importance of these experiences cannot be underestimated.

## Summary: a call to action

This book has argued that freedom needs to be reclaimed by those committed to radical, democratic and/or progressive education, and yet many schools are retreating from the concept and distancing themselves from the phrase. Given this situation, it is imperative that advocates of freedom build a community and work together. At this particular time, being isolated is risky, and many students, teachers, parents, school leaders and informal educators are currently isolated and 'swimming against the tide'. It is vital to build communities and to develop a sense of solidarity. As Davis has argued:

> We fight the same battles over and over again. They are never won for eternity, but in the process of struggling together, in community, we learn how to glimpse new possibilities that otherwise never would have become apparent to us, and in the process we expand and enlarge our very notion of freedom.
>
> (Davis 2012, p. 198)

Freedom needs to be reclaimed by those with radical, democratic and progressive agendas. It needs to be re-conceptualised and re-imagined so that schools and alternative learning spaces feel able to enter into the dialogue and publicly make the case for freedom. There is a central issue in that the notion of 'freedom' is rarely discussed in depth or understood. As Holt (1972, p. 3) argues, 'As a slogan, it is fine. But we don't understand it as a process or mechanism within which people can work and live'. Exploring freedom – and making a case for its advancement – is thus crucial.

This book has argued, through using case examples and stories of radical and progressive practices, that there is another way – a better way – of educating children and young people. The case for offering greater degrees of freedom in education is urgent and compelling. It is essential to work together, as communities of activists – teachers, parents, students, school leaders, informal educators – to present the case for advancing freedom, and to do this alongside a deep-rooted commitment to social justice.

It is time to start to 'sing songs of freedom'. Loudly. Proudly. Confidently. Together.

## Note

1 Ofsted is the national school inspection body in the UK.

## References

Aspy, D.N., and F.N. Roebuck. 1974. "From Humane Ideas to Humane Technology and back Again Many Times." *Education* 95 (2):163–71.

Baginsky, M., and D. Hannam. 1999. *School Councils: The Views of Students and Teachers*. London: NSPCC.

Baker, J., K. Lynch, S. Cantillon, and J. Walsh. 2004. *Equality: From Theory to Action*. Hampshire: Palgrave MacMillan.

Boffey, D. 2015. "Huge shortfall in teachers forces schools to look overseas for new recruits." In *The Guardian*. Available at: www.theguardian.com/education/2015/oct/10/teacher-shortfall-schools-overseas-recruits.

Boud, D. 1988. "Moving Towards Autonomy." In *Developing Student Autonomy in Learning: 2nd Ed*, edited by D. Boud. London: Kogan Page Ltd.

Coffield, F., and B. Williamson. 2011. *From Exam Factories to Communities of Discovery: The Democratic Route*. London: University of London, Institute of Education.

Cornelius-White, J. 2007. "Learner-Centered Teacher-Student Relationships Are Effective: A Meta-Analysis." *Review of Educational Research* 77 (1):113–43.

Crick, B. 2007. "Citizenship: The Political and the Democratic." *British Journal of Educational Studies* 55 (3):235–48.

Davies, L., C. Williams, and H. Yamashita. 2005a. *Inspiring Schools: A Literature Review: Taking up the Challenge of Pupil Participation*. London: Esme Fairburn Foundation and Carnegie UK Trust.

Davies, L., C. Williams, and H. Yamashita. 2005b. *Inspiring Schools: Impact and Outcomes: Taking up the Challenge of Pupil Participation*. London: Esme Fairburn Foundation and Carnegie UK Trust.

Davis, A. 2012. *The Meaning of Freedom*. San Francisco: City Lights Books.

Department for Education. 2013. *Statistical First Release: Permanent and Fixed Period Exclusions from Schools and Exclusion Appeals in England, 2011/12*. London: Department for Education.

Freire, P. 1970. *Pedagogy of the Oppressed*. London: Penguin Books.

Freire, P. 2001. *Pedagogy of Freedom: Ethics, Democracy and Civic Courage*. Maryland: Rowman and Littlefield Publishers Inc.

Gold, J., and T. Gold. 1998. *Learning by Doing*. London: School Councils UK.

Gove, M. 20 June 2011. "Speech on free schools." In *Speech at the Policy Exchange*, London. Available at: www.education.gov.uk/inthenews/speeches/a0077948/michael-goves-speech-to-the-policy-exchange-on-free-schools.

Greenberg, D. 1987. *Free at Last: The Sudbury Valley School*. Massachusetts: Sudbury Valley School Press.

Haimendorf, M., and J. Kestner. 2009. *School Structures – Size Matters*. Bristol: Human Scale Education.

Harber, C. 1996. *Small Schools and Democratic Practice*. Nottingham: Education Heretics Press.

Hecht, Y. 2011. *Democratic Education: A Beginning of a Story*. New York: Alternative Education Resource Organization.

Holt, J. 1972. *Freedom and Beyond*. New York: E.P. Dutton and Company Inc.

hooks, b. 1994. *Teaching to Trangress: Education as the Practice of Freedom*. Oxon: Routledge.

Hope, M.A. 2010. "Trust me, I'm a student: An exploration through Grounded Theory of the student experience in two small schools." University of Hull.

Hope, M.A. 2012a. "Becoming Citizens Through School Experience: A Case Study of Democracy in Practice." *International Journal of Progressive Education* 8 (3):94–109.

Hope, M.A. 2012b. "Small and Perfectly Formed? Is Democracy an Alternative Approach to School Leadership?" *School Leadership and Management* 32 (3):291–305.

Hope, M.A. 2012c. "The Importance of Belonging: Learning from the Student Experience of Democratic Education." *Journal of School Leadership* 22 (4):733–50.

Hope, M.A. 2017. "Re-framing 'Attainment': Creating and Developing Spaces for Learning Within Schools." *FORUM: For Promoting 3–19 Comprehensive Education* 59 (3):413–22.

Hope, M.A. 2018. "Democratic Education in Universities: Pushing at the Boundaries." *Other Education: The Journal of Educational Alternatives* 7 (1):42–5.

Lynch, K., and J. Baker. 2005. "Equality in Education: An Equality of Condition Perspective." *Theory and Research in Education* 3 (2):131–64.

Macmurray, J. 1949. *Conditions of Freedom*. London: Faber and Faber Ltd.

Maitles, H., and R. Deuchar. 2006. "'We Don't Learn Democracy, We Live It!': Consulting the Pupil Voice in Scottish Schools." *Education, Citizenship and Social Justice* 1 (3):249–66.

Maitles, H., and I. Gilchrist. 2006. "Never Too Young to Learn Democracy! A Case Study of a Democratic Approach to Learning in a Religious and Moral Education (RME) Secondary Class in the West of Scotland." *Educational Review* 58 (1):67–85.

Marley, B. 1980. "Redemption Song." In *Island Records*.

Meier, D.W. 1996. "The Big Benefits of Smallness." *Educational Leadership* 54 (1):12–5.

Miller, R. 2002. *Free Schools, Free People: Education and Democracy After the 1960s*. Albany: State University of New York Press.

OECD. 2007. *Understanding the Social Outcomes of Learning*. Paris: OECD Publishing.

Parsons, C. 2005. "School Exclusions in the UK: Numbers, Trends and Variations." In *The RoutledgeFalmer Reader in Inclusive Education*, edited by K. Topping and S. Maloney. Oxon: Routledge.

Reay, D. 2012. "What Would a Socially Just Education System Look Like? Saving the Minnows from the Pike." *Journal of Education Policy* 27 (5):587–99.

Rogers, C. 1980. *A Way of Being*. Boston: Houghton Mifflin Company.

Rowling, J.K. 2003. *Harry Potter and the Order of the Phoenix*. London: Bloomsbury.

Säfström, C.A., and G. Biesta. 2011. "A Manifesto for Education." *Policy Futures in Education* 9 (5):540–7.

Schumacher, E.F. 1993. *Small Is Beautiful*. London: Vintage (first published 1973).

*United Nations*. 1989. "Convention on the Rights of the Child." Office of the High Commissioner. Accessed 20/03/18. Available at: www.ohchr.org/EN/Professional Interest/Pages/CRC.aspx.

Van Parijs, P. 1995/2007. "Real Freedom for All (1995)." In *Freedom: A Philosophical Anthology*, edited by I. Carter, M.H. Kramer and H. Steiner. Oxford: Blackwell Publishing.

Vaughan, M. 2006. *Summerhill and A.S. Neill*. Berks: Open University Press.

Wallace, W. 2009. *Schools Within Schools: Human Scale Education in Practice*. London: Calouste Gulbenkian Foundation.

Wiborg, S., F. Green, P. Taylor-Gooby, and R.J. Wilde. 2018. "Free Schools in England: 'Not Unlike other Schools'?" *Journal of Social Policy* 47 (1):119–37.

*Youth Employment UK*. "The Youth Employment UK: Employability Review." Accessed 17/04/2018. Available at: www.youthemployment.org.uk/dev/wp-content/uploads/2017/07/Youth-Employment-UK-Employability-Review-June-2017.pdf.

# Index

Note: Bold page references indicate tables on the corresponding pages.